# EASIEST
# KEYBOARD
# COLLECTION

# Pop
# Chart Hits

**WISE PUBLICATIONS**
London/New York/Paris/Sydney/Copenhagen/Madrid/Tokyo

Exclusive Distributors:

**Music Sales Limited**
8/9 Frith Street,
London W1V 5TZ, England.

**Music Sales Pty Limited**
120 Rothschild Avenue,
Rosebery, NSW 2018,
Australia.

Order No. AM959893
ISBN 0-7119-7789-5
This book © Copyright 2000 by Wise Publications

Book design by Chloë Alexander
Compiled by Nick Crispin
Music arranged by Roger Day and Derek Jones
Music processed by Paul Ewers Music Design
Cover photograph courtesy of REX Features

Printed in the United Kingdom by
The Bath Press, Bath

**Your Guarantee of Quality**
As publishers, we strive to produce every book to the highest
commercial standards. This book has been carefully designed to
minimise awkward page turns and to make playing from it a real
pleasure. Particular care has been given to specifying acid-free,
neutral-sized paper made from pulps which have not been elemental
chlorine bleached. This pulp is from farmed sustainable forests and
was produced with special regard for the environment. Throughout,
the printing and binding have been planned to ensure a sturdy,
attractive publication which should give years of enjoyment. If your
copy fails to meet our high standards, please inform us and we will
gladly replace it.

Music Sales' complete catalogue describes thousands of titles and is
available in full colour sections by subject, direct from Music Sales
Limited. Please state your areas of interest and send a cheque/postal
order for £1.50 for postage to: Music Sales Limited, Newmarket Road,
Bury St. Edmunds, Suffolk IP33 3YB.

www.musicsales.com

# Contents

# A DIFFERENT BEAT

*Words & Music by Martin Brannigan, Stephen Gately,*
*Ronan Keating, Shane Lynch, Ray Hedges & Keith Duffy*

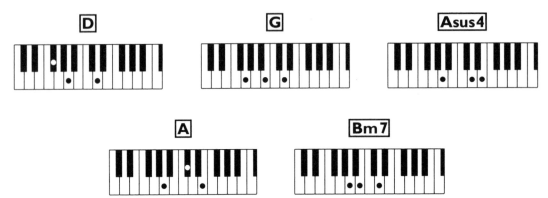

Voice:   **Piano**

Rhythm:   **Soft Rock**

Tempo:   ♩ = 88

Let's not for - get this place, ___ let's not ne - glect our race, ___ let u - ni-

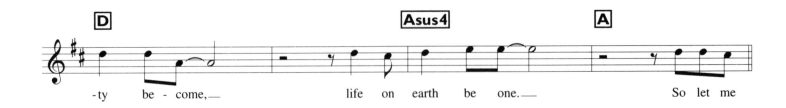

-ty be - come, ___ life on earth be one. ___ So let me

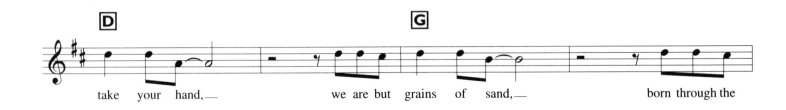

take your hand, ___ we are but grains of sand, ___ born through the

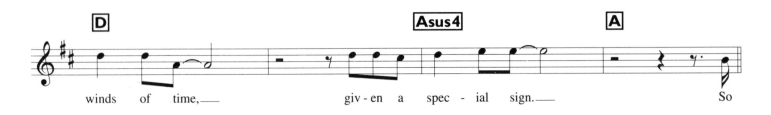

winds of time, ___ giv - en a spec - ial sign. ___ So

let's take a stand and look a - round us now, peo - ple._____ So

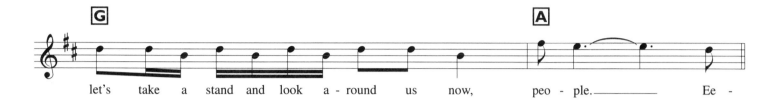

let's take a stand and look a - round us now, peo - ple._____ Ee -

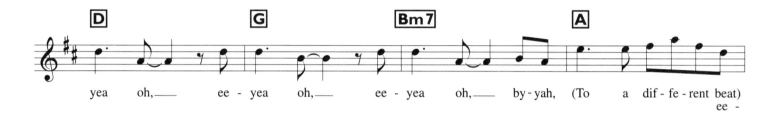

yea oh,___ ee - yea oh,___ ee - yea oh,___ by - yah, (To a dif - fe - rent beat) ee -

- yea oh,___ ee - yea oh,___ ee - yea oh,___ by - yah.___

How___ far___ we've come___ and how___ far___ to go.

Rain___ does___ not fall___ on one___ roof___ a -

- lone.
(To a dif - fe - rent beat)

# ...BABY ONE MORE TIME

**Words & Music by Max Martin**

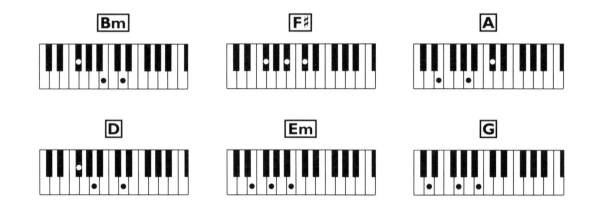

Voice: **Piano 1**

Rhythm: **Pop Ballad**

Tempo: ♩ = **96**

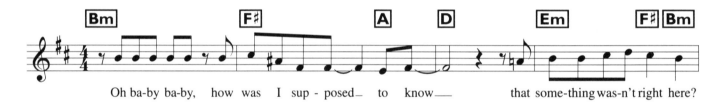

Oh ba-by ba-by, how was I sup-posed— to know— that some-thing was-n't right here?

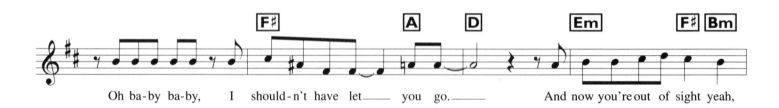

Oh ba-by ba-by, I should-n't have let— you go.— And now you're out of sight yeah,

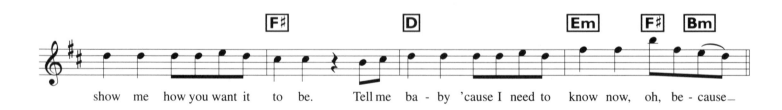

show me how you want it to be. Tell me ba-by 'cause I need to know now, oh, be-cause—

my lone-li-ness is kill-ing me and— I,— I must con-fess I still be-lieve,— still be-lieve.

When I'm not with you I lose my mind, give me a sign,⎯ hit me ba - by one more time.

Oh ba - by ba - by, how was I sup - posed⎯ to know?⎯

Oh pret - ty ba - by I should - n't have let⎯ you go.⎯ I must con - fess⎯

⎯ that my lone - li - ness⎯ is kill - ing me now.⎯ Don't you know I⎯ still⎯ be - lieve

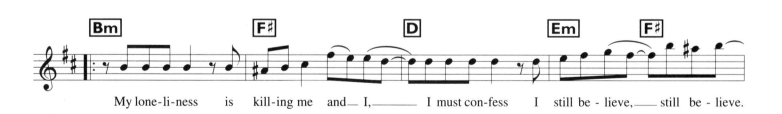

⎯ that you will be here⎯ and give me a sign.⎯ Hit me ba - by one more time.

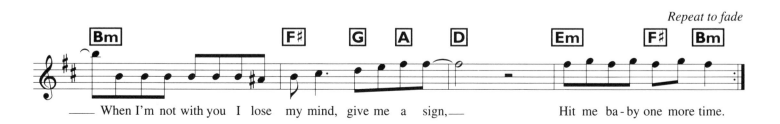

My lone - li - ness is kill - ing me and⎯ I,⎯ I must con - fess I still be - lieve,⎯ still be - lieve.

*Repeat to fade*

When I'm not with you I lose my mind, give me a sign,⎯ Hit me ba - by one more time.

# BARBIE GIRL

*Words & Music by Soren Rasted, Claus Norreen, Rene Dif,*
*Lene Nystrom, Johnny Pederson & Karsten Delgado*

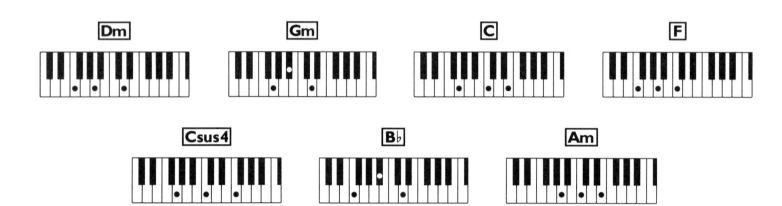

Voice:    **Clarinet**

Rhythm:   **Rock**

Tempo:    ♩ = 136

I'm a blonde bim-bo girl in a fan-

-ta-sy world, dress me up, make it tight, I'm your dol-ly. You're my doll,

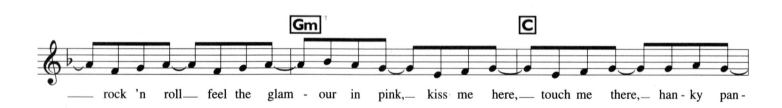

rock 'n roll feel the glam-our in pink, kiss me here, touch me there, han-ky pan-

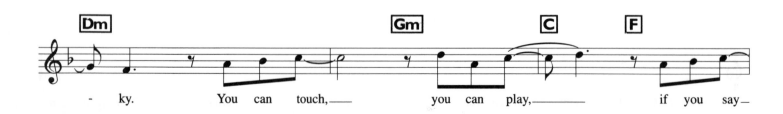

-ky. You can touch, you can play, if you say

I'm al - ways yours._____ I'm a Bar - bie girl

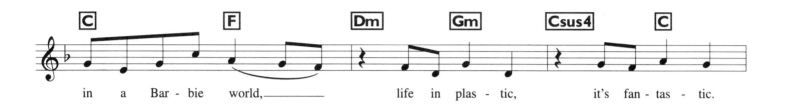

in a Bar - bie world,_____ life in plas - tic, it's fan - tas - tic.

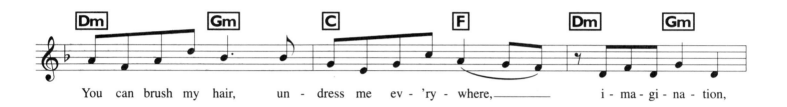

You can brush my hair, un - dress me ev - 'ry - where,_____ i - ma - gi - na - tion,

life is your cre - a - tion.__ Come on Bar - bie, let's go par - ty. Ah ah ah yeah.__

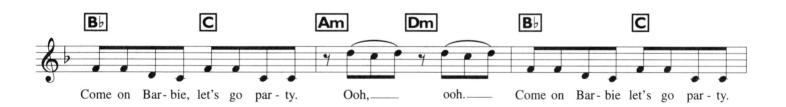

Come on Bar - bie, let's go par - ty. Ooh,____ ooh.____ Come on Bar - bie let's go par - ty.

Ah ah ah yeah.__ Come on Bar - bie, let's go par - ty. Ooh,_____ ooh._____

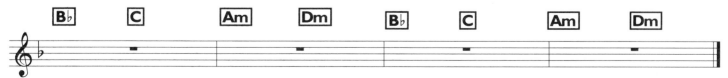

*Spoken:* Ooh I'm having so much fun! Well Barbie, we're just getting started. Ooh, I love you Ken!

# BIG MISTAKE

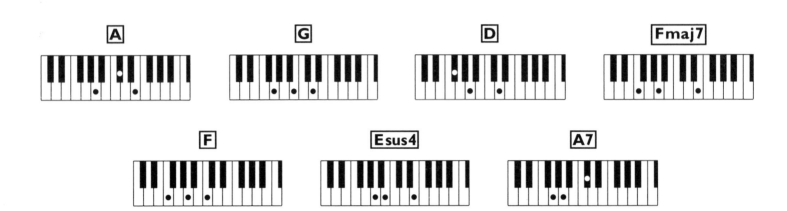

Voice:  **Electric Piano I**

Rhythm:  **Pop Ballad**

Tempo:  ♩ = 92

There's no sign— on the gate,— and there's mud— on your face,—

don't you think— it's time we re-in-ves-ti-gate this si-tu-a-tion.

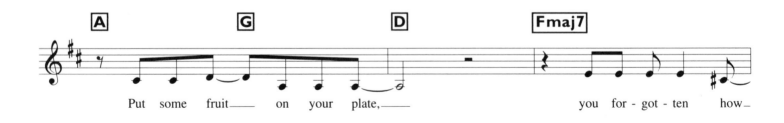

Put some fruit— on your plate,— you for-got-ten how—

—— it start-ed, close your eyes, think of all the bub-bles of love we made.

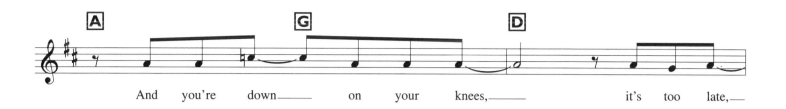
And you're down_____ on your knees,_____ it's too late,_____

_____ oh don't come crawl - ing. And you lie_____ by my feet,_____

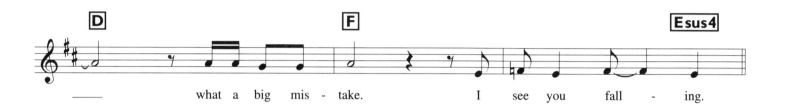
_____ what a big mis - take. I see you fall - ing.

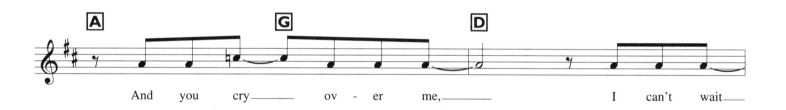
And you cry_____ ov - er me,_____ I can't wait_____

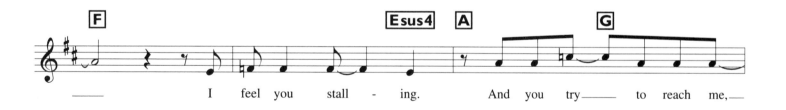
_____ I feel you stall - ing. And you try_____ to reach me,_____

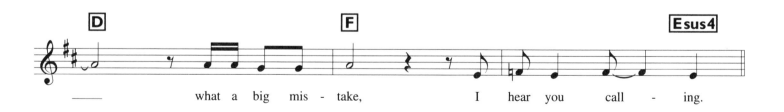
_____ what a big mis - take, I hear you call - ing.

*Repeat to fade*

11

# BLAME IT ON THE WEATHERMAN

***Words & Music by Ray Hedges, Martin Brannigan, Andy Caine & Tracy Ackerman***
© Copyright 1998 19 Music Limited/BMG Music Publishing Limited, Bedford House, 69-79 Fulham High Street, London SW6 (25%),
Universal Music Publishing Limited, 77 Fulham Palace Road, London W6 (25%), Palan Music Publishing Limited, Greenland Place,
115-123 Bayham Street, London NW1 (25%) & Chrysalis Music Limited, The Chrysalis Building, Bramley Road, London W10 (25%).
This arrangement © 1999 Copyright BMG Music Publishing Limited for their share of interest.

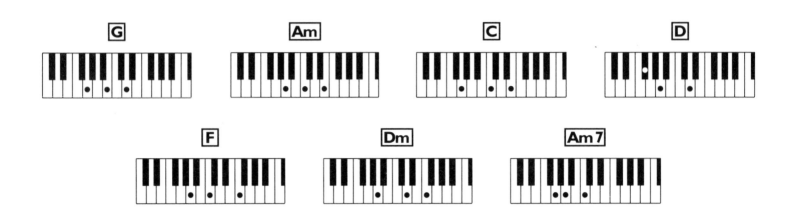

Voice:     **Alto Saxophone**

Rhythm:    **Soft Rock 1**

Tempo:     ♩ = 94

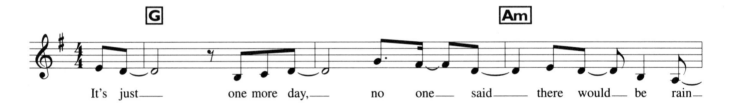

It's just____  one more day,____  no one____ said____ there would__ be  rain__

____ a-gain,  won't blame it on my-self,  yeah.  I'll blame it on  the  wea-ther-man.__ Stand-ing on the

shore  call-ing  out  your  name,  I  was  here  be-fore____  I  could  see  your

face,  on - ly  clouds  will  see  tears  are  in  my  eyes,____  em - pty  like  my

heart, why d'ya say good - bye?\_\_\_\_\_ The rain goes

on, on\_\_\_\_\_ and on a - gain.\_\_\_ The rain goes on, on\_\_\_\_\_ and

on a - gain.\_\_\_ The rain goes on, on\_\_\_\_\_ and on a - gain.\_\_\_ May - be it's too late,

may - be it's too late to start a - gain.\_\_\_ May - be I can't pray.

May - be I can't wait, may - be I can't blame the wea - ther - man.\_\_\_ The rain goes

on, on\_\_\_\_\_ and on a - gain.\_\_\_ The rain goes on, on\_\_\_\_\_ and on a - gain.\_\_\_ The rain goes

on, on\_\_\_\_\_ and on a - gain.\_\_\_ Oh blame it on the wea - ther - man.\_\_\_

# BRING IT ALL BACK

*Words & Music by Eliot Kennedy, Mike Percy, Tim Lever & S Club 7*
© Copyright 1999 19 Music Limited/BMG Music Publishing Limited,
Bedford House, 69-79 Fulham High Street, London SW6 (53.32%),
Sony/ATV Music Publishing (UK) Limited, 10 Great Marlborough Street, London W1 (26.66%) &
Universal Music Publishing Limited, 77 Fulham Palace Road, London W6 (20.02%).
All Rights Reserved. International Copyright Secured.

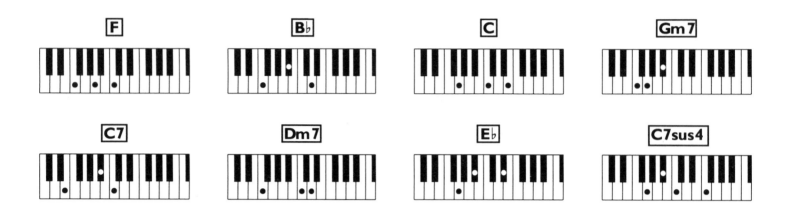

Voice: **Tenor Saxophone**

Rhythm: **Funky Pop 2**

Tempo: ♩ = 108

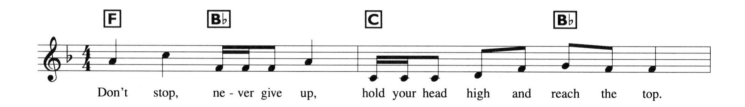

Don't stop, ne-ver give up, hold your head high and reach the top.

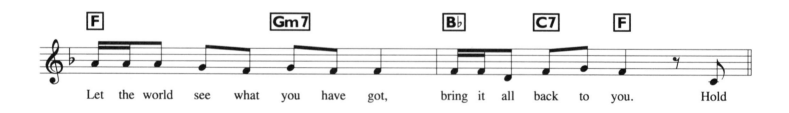

Let the world see what you have got, bring it all back to you. Hold

on to what— you try to be, your in-di-vi-du-a-li-ty. When the

world is on your shoul-ders, just smile and let it go. If

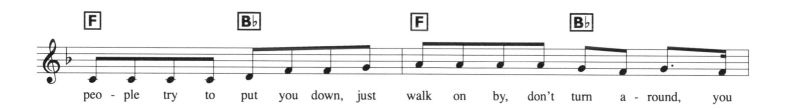

peo - ple try to put you down, just walk on by, don't turn a - round, you

on - ly have to ans - wer to your - self. Don't you know it's true what they say, in

life it ain't ea - sy, but your time's com - ing a - round.— So don't you stop try - ing.

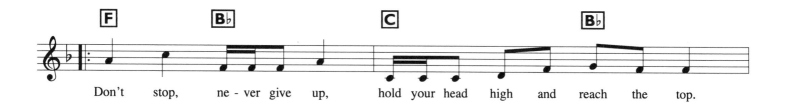

Don't stop, ne - ver give up, hold your head high and reach the top.

Let the world see what you have got, bring it all back to you.

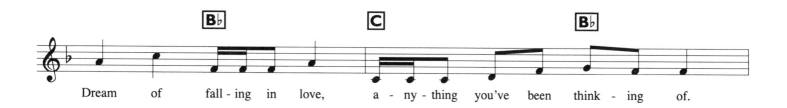

Dream of fall - ing in love, a - ny - thing you've been think - ing of.

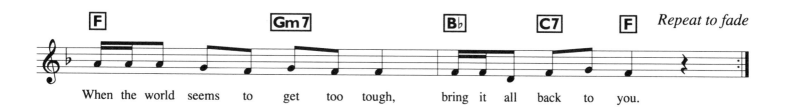

When the world seems to get too tough, bring it all back to you.

# COMMON PEOPLE

*Music by Pulp*
*Lyrics by Jarvis Cocker*

Voice: **Electric Piano**

Rhythm: **Pop Rock**

Tempo: ♩ = 150

She came from Greece, she had a thirst for know-ledge,

she stu-died sculp-ture at St. Mar-tin's col-lege, that's where I___

___ caught her eye.___

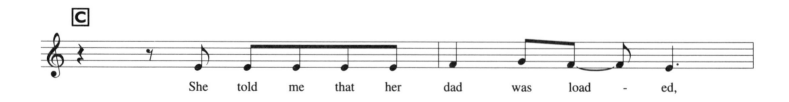

She told me that her dad was load-ed,

I said "In that case I'll have rum and Co-ca Co-la." She said "Fine."___

And then in thir - ty se - conds time,_____ she said

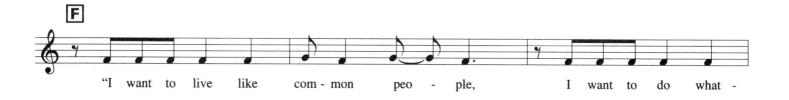
**F**
"I want to live like com - mon peo - ple, I want to do what -

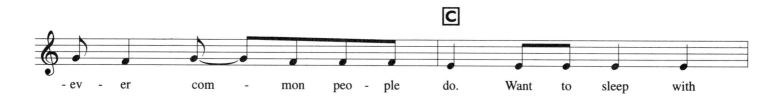
**C**
- ev - er com - mon peo - ple do. Want to sleep with

com - mon peo - ple, I want to sleep with com - mon peo - ple like you."

**G7**
_____ Well what else_____ could I do?_____ I said I'll...

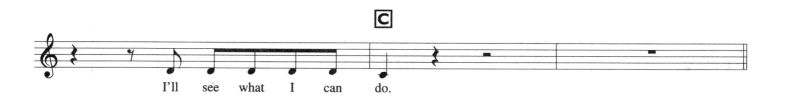
**C**
I'll see what I can do.

*Repeat to fade*

Want to live like com - mon peo - ple like you.

# FALLING INTO YOU

**Words & Music by Rick Nowels, Marie-Claire D'Ubaldo & Billy Steinberg**

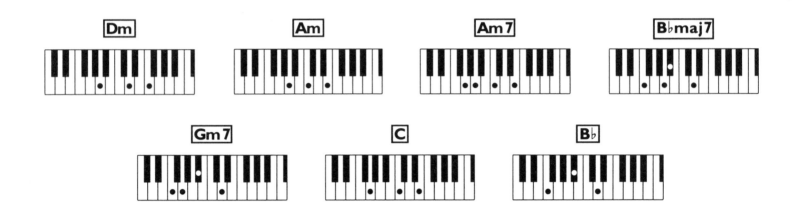

Voice: **Clarinet**

Rhythm: **Pop Ballad**

Tempo: ♩ = 104

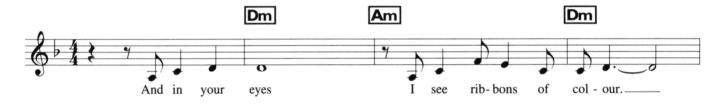

And in your eyes I see rib-bons of col-our.

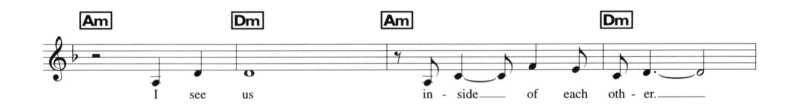

I see us in-side of each oth-er.

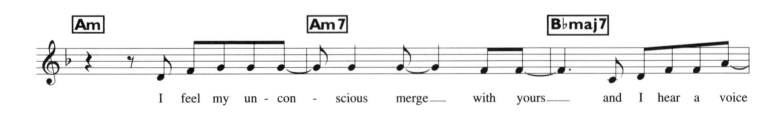

I feel my un-con-scious merge with yours and I hear a voice

say, "What's his is hers." I'm fall-ing in-to

you. This dream could come true, and it feels

so good fall - ing in - to you. Fall - ing like a leaf,

fall - ing like a star,

find - ing a be - lief fall - ing where

you are. Fall -

- ing in - to you, fall - ing in - to you,

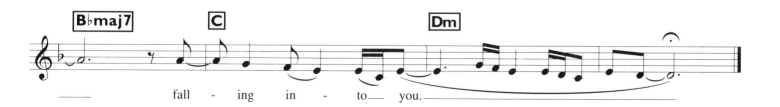

fall - ing in - to you.

# FEMALE OF THE SPECIES

*Words & Music by Tommy Scott, James Edwards, Francis Griffiths & Andrew Parle*
© Copyright 1996 Hit & Run Music (Publishing) Limited, 30 Ives Street, London SW3.
All Rights Reserved. International Copyright Secured.

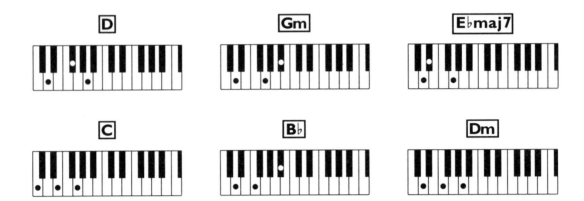

Voice: **Distortion Guitar**

Rhythm: **8 Beat Pop**

Tempo: ♩ = 112

A thou - sand thun - der - ing thrills a - wait___ me,

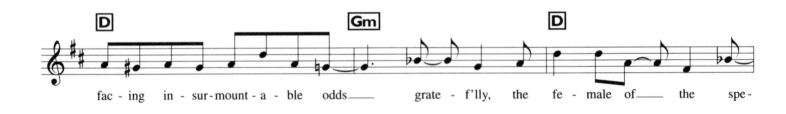

fac - ing in - sur - mount - a - ble odds___ grate - f'lly, the fe - male of___ the spe-

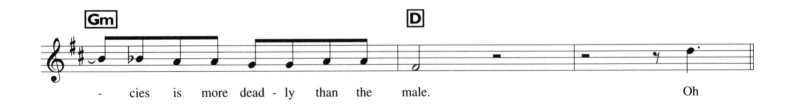

- cies is more dead - ly than the male. Oh

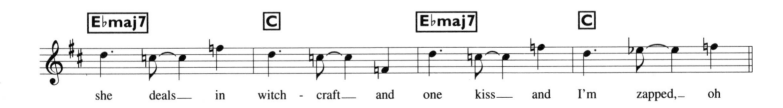

she deals___ in witch - craft___ and one kiss___ and I'm zapped,___ oh

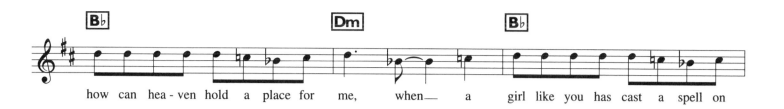

how can hea-ven hold a place for me, when— a girl like you has cast a spell on

me, oh,———— how can hea-ven hold a place for me when— a

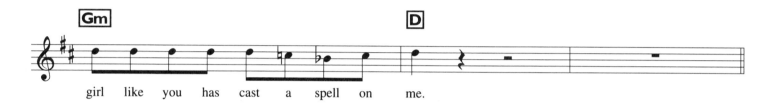

girl like you has cast a spell on me.

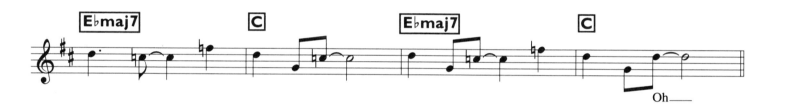

Oh——

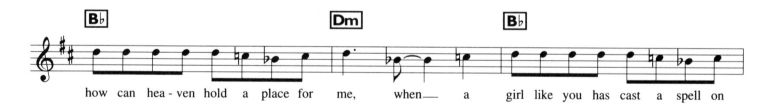

how can hea-ven hold a place for me, when— a girl like you has cast a spell on

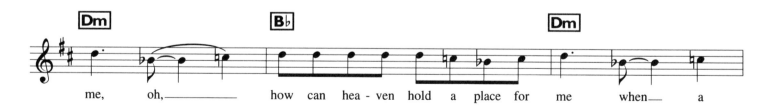

me, oh,———— how can hea-ven hold a place for me when— a

girl like you has cast a spell on me.

21

# GOOD ENOUGH

**Words & Music by Nigel Clark, Mathew Priest & Andy Miller**
© Copyright 1996 BMG Music Publishing Limited, Bedford House, 69-79 Fulham High Street, London SW6.
This arrangement © Copyright 1997 BMG Music Publishing Limited.
All Rights Reserved. International Copyright Secured.

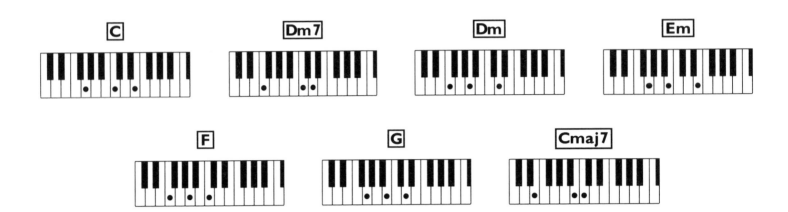

Voice: **Saxophone**

Rhythm: **Rock**

Tempo: ♩ = 116

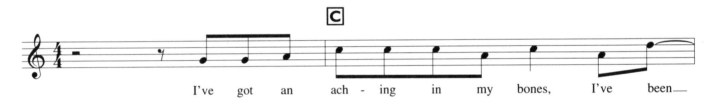

I've got an ach - ing in my bones, I've been __

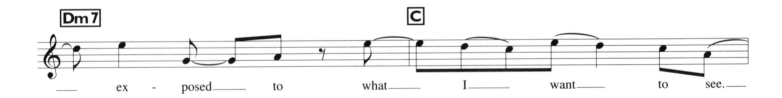

__ ex - posed __ to     what __ I __ want __ to see.

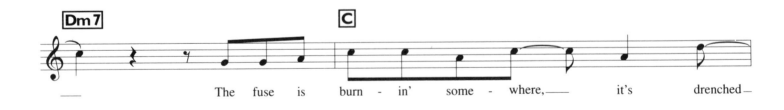

__ The fuse is burn - in' some - where, __ it's     drenched __

__ in heat,     it's     where __ I __ long __ to be.

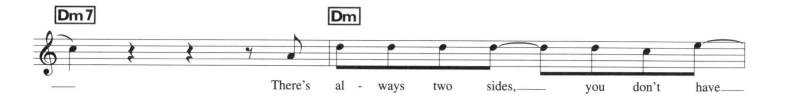

**Dm 7**        **Dm**

—— There's al - ways two sides,—— you don't have——

**Em**        **F**

—— to suf - fer, if this is hea - ven then send me—— to

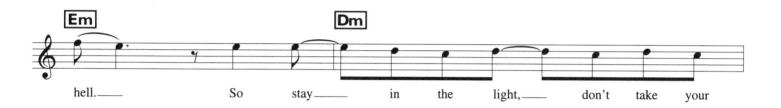

**Em**        **Dm**

hell.—— So stay—— in the light,—— don't take your

**Em**        **F**        **G**

eyes from the prize.—— Hey!—— There goes the bell.—— If it's

**Cmaj7**        **Dm 7**        **Cmaj7**

good e - nough for you, it's good—— e - nough for me. If it's good—— e - nough it's true, it's what——

**Dm 7**        **Cmaj7**        **Dm 7**

—— I want to see. If it's good e - nough for you, it's good—— e - nough for me. If it's good

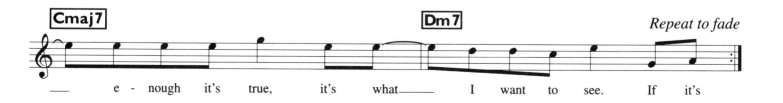

**Cmaj7**        **Dm 7**        *Repeat to fade*

—— e - nough it's true, it's what—— I want to see. If it's

# HAVE I TOLD YOU LATELY

**Words & Music by Van Morrison**

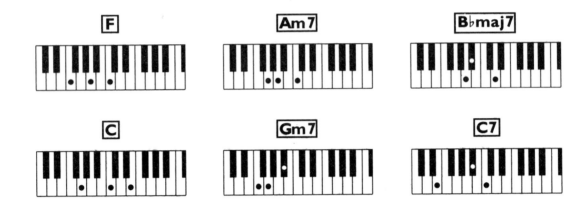

Voice:   **Flute**

Rhythm:   **Ballad**

Tempo:   ♩ = 80

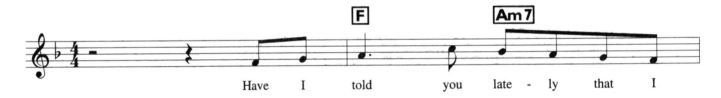

Have   I   told   you   late-ly   that   I

love____ you,____   have   I   told   you   there's   no - one____ a-

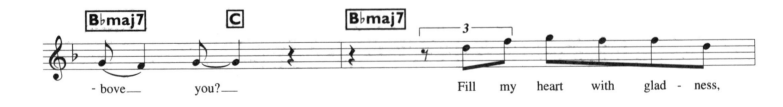

- bove____ you?____   Fill   my   heart   with   glad - ness,

take a-way   my   sad-ness,   ease   my   trou-bles   that's   what   you   do.

There's a love that's di - vine and it's yours and it's mine, like the

sun.

At the end of the day, we should give thanks and pray to the one.

Have I told you late - ly that I love you,

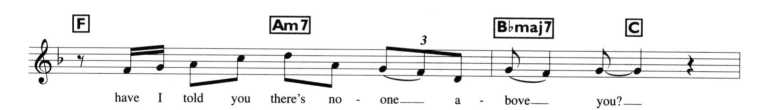
have I told you there's no - one a - bove you?

Fill my heart with glad - ness, take a - way my sad - ness,

ease my trou - bles that's what you do.

# I BELIEVE I CAN FLY

**Words & Music by R. Kelly**

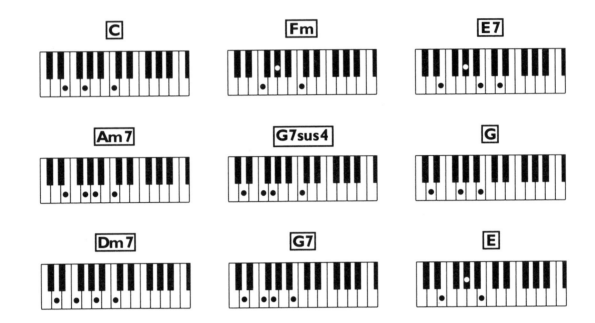

Voice: **Vibraphone**

Rhythm: **Soul Ballad**

Tempo: ♩ = 69

I used to think— that I could not— go on. and

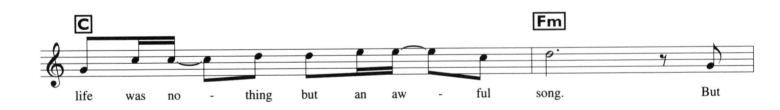

life was no - thing but an aw - ful song. But

now I know— the mean - ing of— true love,———— I'm

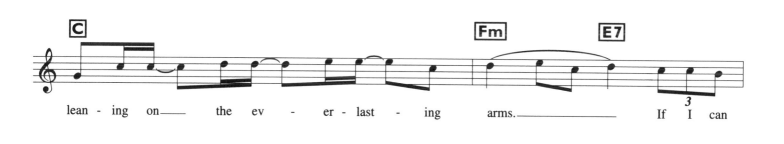

lean - ing on —— the ev - er - last - ing arms. —————— If I can

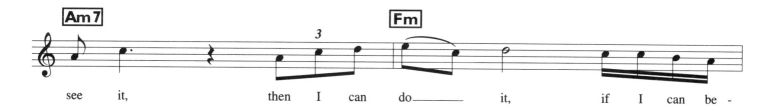

see it, then I can do —— it, if I can be -

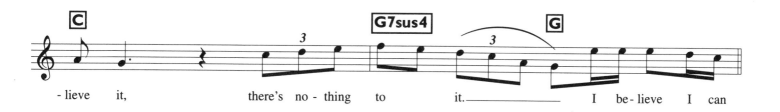

- lieve it, there's no - thing to it. —————— I be - lieve I can

fly, I be - lieve I can touch the sky. —— I think a - bout it ev - 'ry

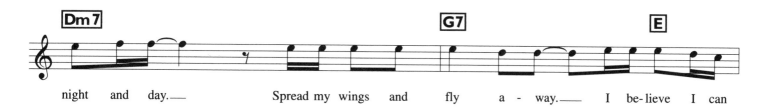

night and day. —— Spread my wings and fly a - way. —— I be - lieve I can

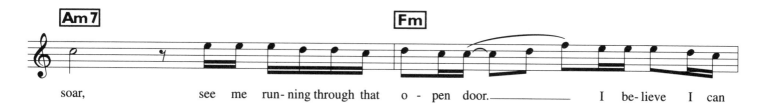

soar, see me run - ning through that o - pen door. —————— I be - lieve I can

fly, I be - lieve I can fly, I be - lieve —— I can fly.

# I'LL BE MISSING YOU

***Words & Music by Sting***
***Additional Words by T. Gaither & F. Evans***
© Copyright 1983 G.M. Sumner.
EMI Music Publishing Limited/Magnetic Publishing Limited.
All Rights Reserved. International Copyright Secured.

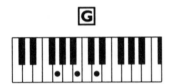
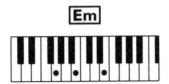
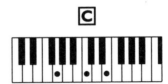
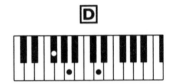

Voice: **Flute**

Rhythm: **Soft Rock**

Tempo: ♩ = 116

Ev - 'ry step I_____ take,

ev - 'ry move I_____ make,

ev - 'ry sin - gle day,_____ ev - 'ry time_____ I pray_____

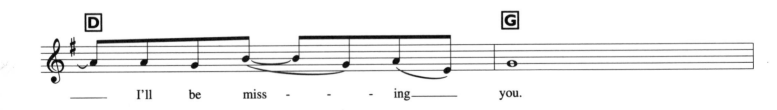

_____ I'll be miss - - - ing_____ you.

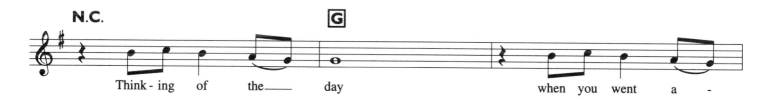

Think-ing of the____ day when you went a-

way, what a life____ to take,____ what I'm bound____ to break,-

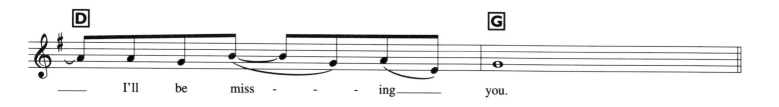

____ I'll be miss - - - ing____ you.

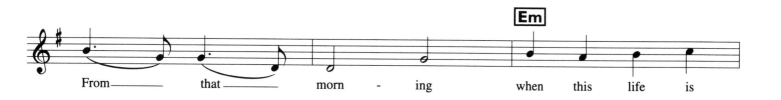

From____ that____ morn - ing when this life is

ov - - er, I____ know____ I'll____ see your

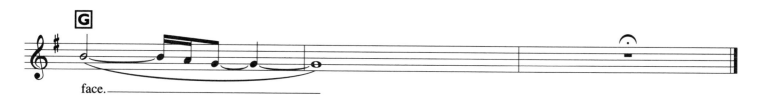

face.____

# I'M YOUR ANGEL

*Words & Music by R. Kelly*

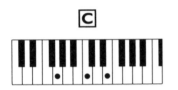 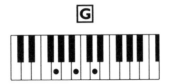 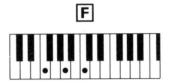 

  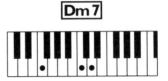

Voice: **Gut Guitar**

Rhythm: **Soul Ballad**

Tempo: ♩ = 108

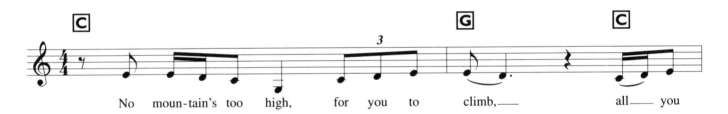

No moun-tain's too high, for you to climb, all you

have to do is have some climb-ing faith oh yeah.

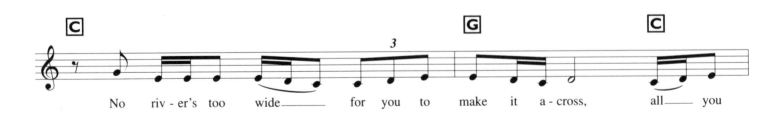

No riv-er's too wide for you to make it a-cross, all you

have to do is be-lieve it when you pray. And

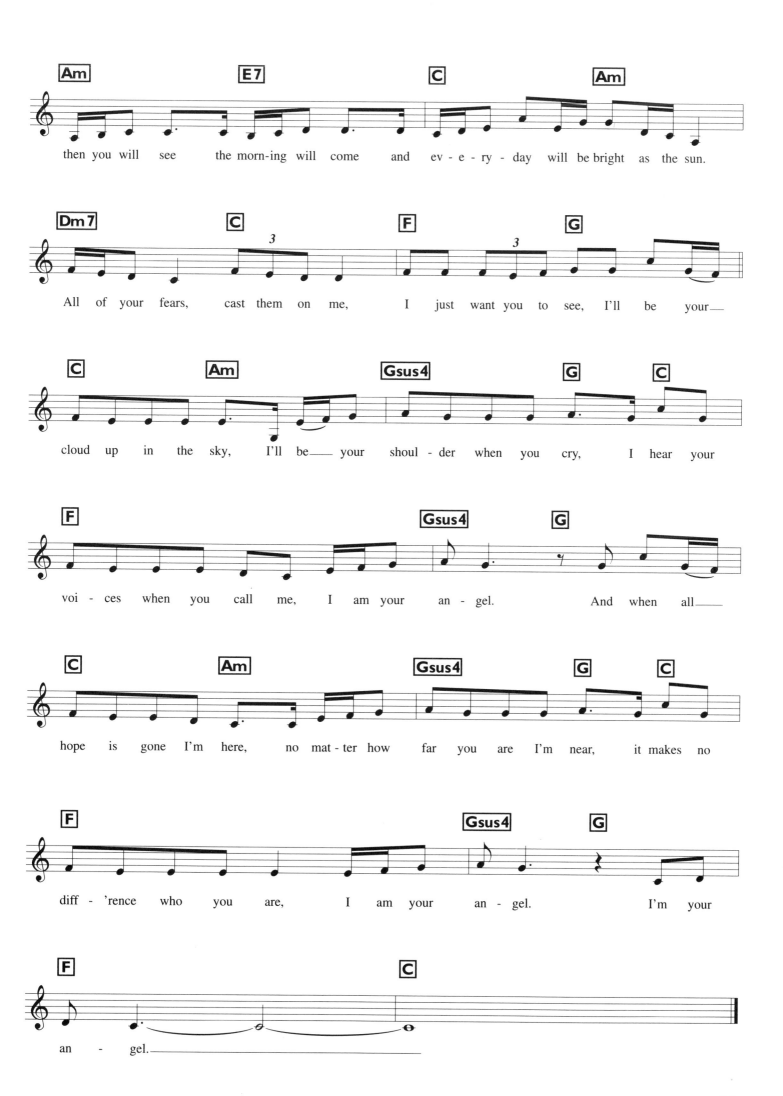

# IRONIC

**Music by Alanis Morissette & Glenn Ballard**
**Words by Alanis Morissette**

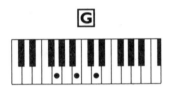 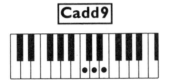 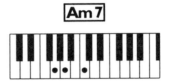 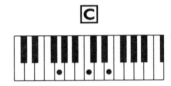

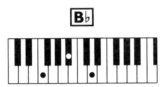 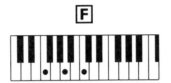 

Voice:  **Soprano Saxophone**

Rhythm:  **Soft Rock 3**

Tempo:  ♩ = 110

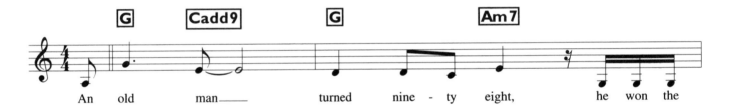

An old man turned nine - ty eight, he won the

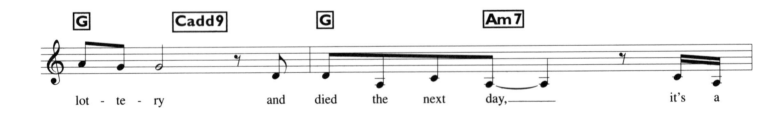

lot - te - ry and died the next day, it's a

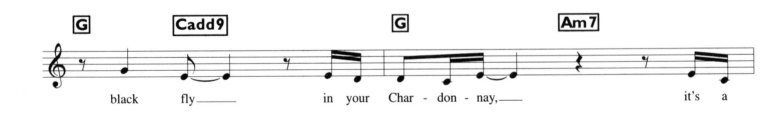

black fly in your Char - don - nay, it's a

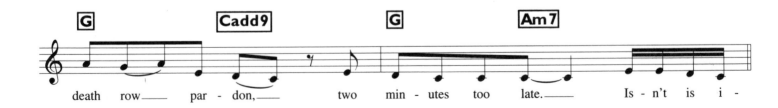

death row par - don, two min - utes too late. Is - n't is i-

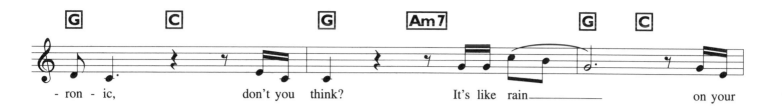

- ron - ic, don't you think? It's like rain_____ on your

wed - ding day.____ It's a free____ ride,_____ when you're al - rea - dy paid,___ it's the good ad -

- vice, that you just did - n't take,___ who would - 've thought___ it fig -

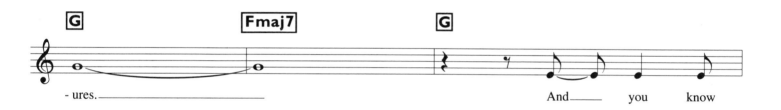

- ures._____ And____ you know

life has a fun - ny way of sneak - ing up on you._____

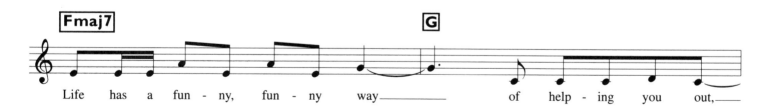

Life has a fun - ny, fun - ny way____ of help - ing you out,___

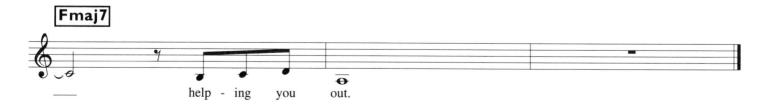

____ help - ing you out.

# LAST THING ON MY MIND

***Words by Sarah Dallin & Keren Woodward***
***Music by Mike Stock & Pete Waterman***

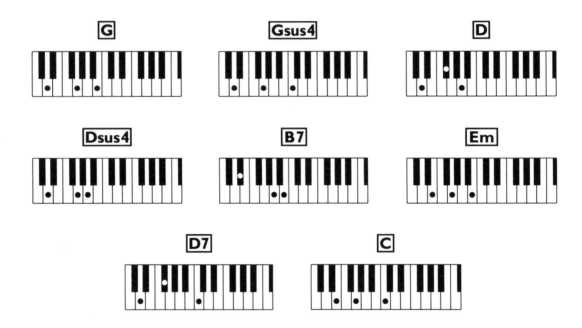

Voice:   **Studio Piano**
Rhythm:  **Lite Pop**
Tempo:   ♩ = 124

There was some - thing in___ your___ voice___ that was tell-

- ing me___ don't be too sure,___ a - rous-ing my___ sus - pi - cions, I have ne -

- ver felt___ be - fore.___ I thought we had___ it made,___

I thought you'd ne - ver go_____ a - way.____ But now you're

sud - den - ly like____ a stran - ger, and you're leav - ing our love____ be - hind,__

____ of all the things____ I was ev - er plan - ning for,__

this was____ the last____ thing_ on____ my mind. Ah,_____ ah,__

____ ah.____ But now you're sud - den - ly like____ a stran - ger and you're

leav - ing our love____ be - hind,____ of all the things____ I was ev - er

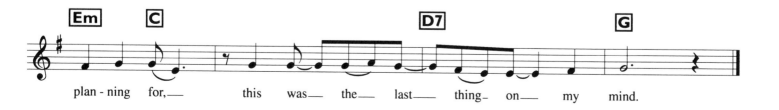

plan - ning for,__ this was____ the____ last____ thing_ on____ my mind.

# LIVIN' LA VIDA LOCA

**Words & Music by Desmond Child & Robi Rosa**
*© Copyright 1999 Desmophobia/Universal Music Publishing Limited,*
*77 Fulham Palace Road, London W6 (50%) & A Phantom Vox Publishing/*
*Muziekuitgeverij Artemis/Warner Chappell Music Limited, Griffin House,*
*161 Hammersmith Road, London W6 (50%).*

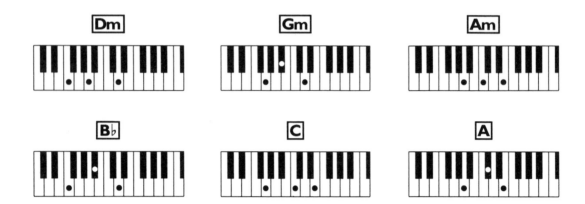

Voice:     **Piano 2**

Rhythm:   **Samba**

Tempo:    ♩ = 88

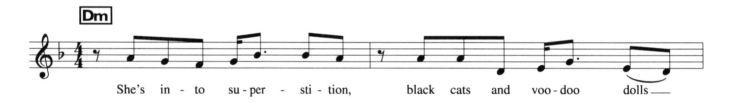

She's in-to su-per-sti-tion, black cats and voo-doo dolls

and I feel a pre-mo-ni-tion, that girl's gon-na make me fall.

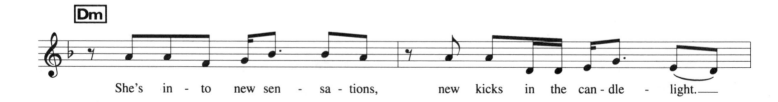

She's in-to new sen-sa-tions, new kicks in the can-dle-light.

She's got a new ad-dic-tion s'full ev-'ry day and night. She'll make you take your clothes off and go

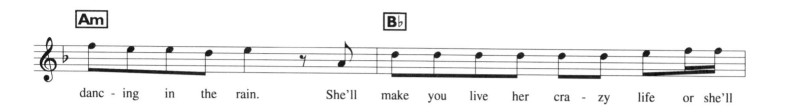

danc-ing in the rain. She'll make you live her cra-zy life or she'll

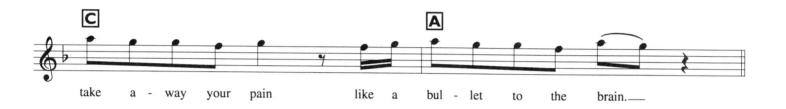

take a-way your pain like a bul-let to the brain.

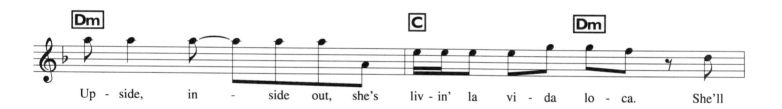

Up-side, in-side out, she's liv-in' la vi-da lo-ca. She'll

push and pull you down, liv-in' la vi-da lo-ca. Her lips are dev-il red and her

skin's the co-lour of mo-cha. She will wear you out, liv-in' la vi-da lo-ca,

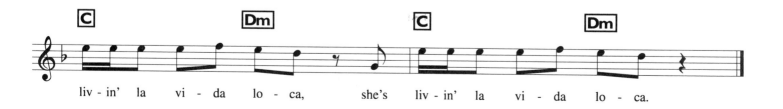

liv-in' la vi-da lo-ca, she's liv-in' la vi-da lo-ca.

# MAMBO No.5 (A LITTLE BIT OF...)

*Music by Perez 'Prez' Prado*
*Words by Lou Bega & Zippy*

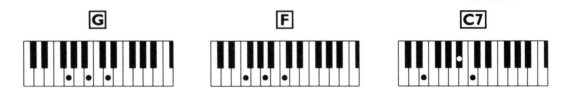

Voice: **Trumpet**

Rhythm: **Swing**

Tempo: ♩ = 172

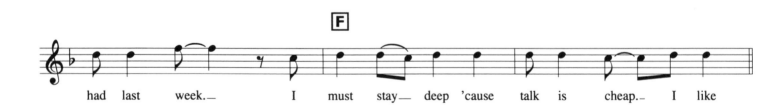

a lit - tle bit of Ri - ta's all I need,___ a lit - tle bit of

Ti - na's what I see.___ A lit - tle bit of San - dra in the sun,___

a lit - tle bit of Ma - ry all night long,___

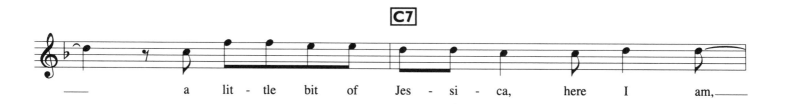

a lit - tle bit of Jes - si - ca, here I am,___

a lit - tle bit of you makes me your man.___

# MAN! I FEEL LIKE A WOMAN!

**Words & Music by Shania Twain & Robert John "Mutt" Lange**
© Copyright 1997 Out Of Pocket Productions Limited &
Loon Echo Incorporated/Songs Of PolyGram International Incorporated, USA.
Zomba Music Publishers Limited, 165-167 High Road, London NW10 (50%)/
Universal Music Publishing Limited, 77 Fulham Palace Road, London W6 (50%).
All Rights Reserved. International Copyright Secured.

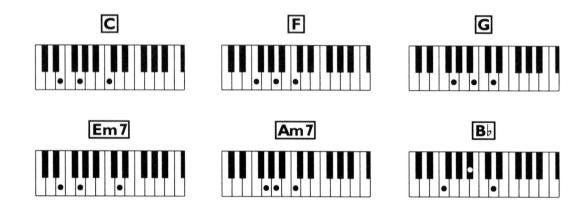

Voice: **Electric Guitar**

Rhythm: **Chicago Blues**

Tempo: ♩ = 120

I'm go - - ing out to - night, I'm feel - ing al - right, gon -

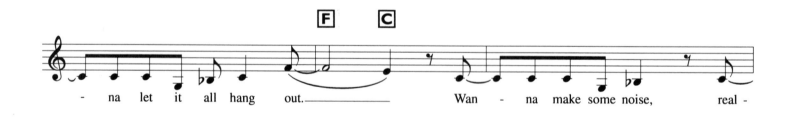

- na let it all hang out. ___ Wan - na make some noise, real -

- ly raise my voice, yeah, ___ I wan - na scream and shout.

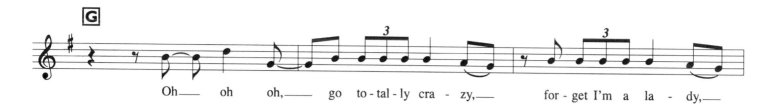
Oh— oh oh,— go to-tal-ly cra - zy,— for-get I'm a la - dy,—

men's shirts, short skirts. Oh— oh oh,— real-ly go wild, yeah,—

do - ing it in style.— Oh— oh oh,— get in the ac - tion,—

feel the at - trac - tion,— co - lour my hair, what do I dare?

Oh— oh oh,— I wan - na be free, yeah, to

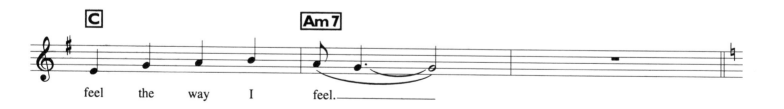
feel the way I feel.—

I feel like a wo - man.

# MARVELLOUS

*Words & Music by Ian Broudie*

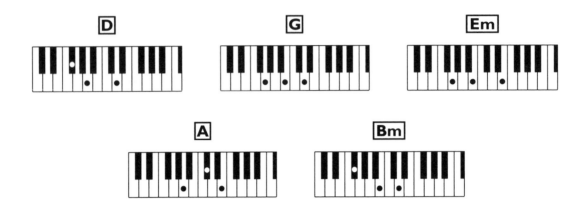

Voice: **Studio Piano**

Rhythm: **Dance Pop 1**

Tempo: ♩ = 132

Oh—— you hope to fit but you're fit to drop,

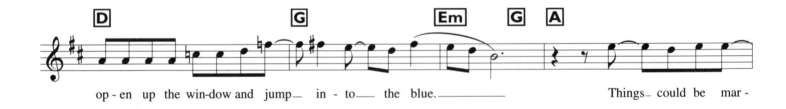

op - en up the win-dow and jump—— in - to—— the blue.—————— Things— could be mar-

- vel - lous, things—— could be fa - bu-lous.

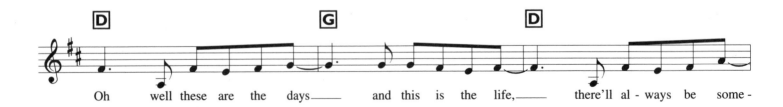

Oh well these are the days—— and this is the life,—— there'll al - ways be some-

- thing on your mind, _____ you'll nev - er quite find,

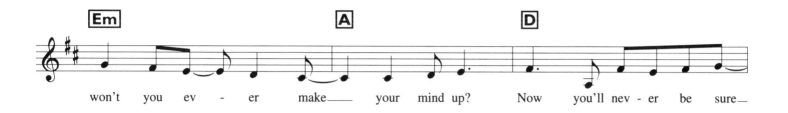

won't you ev - er make _____ your mind up? Now you'll nev - er be sure _____

_____ if this is the time, _____ if this is the mo - ment, the end of the line, _____

_____ you'll nev - er de - cide, you used to know _____ but now _____

_____ you've for - got - ten, a sub - ma - rine _____ got stuck _____ to the bot - tom,

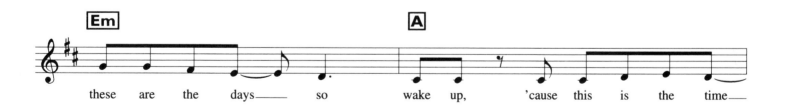

these are the days _____ so wake up, 'cause this is the time _____

_____ and you know _____ I'm _____ right.

# MI CHICO LATINO

**Words & Music by Geri Halliwell, Andy Watkins & Paul Wilson**

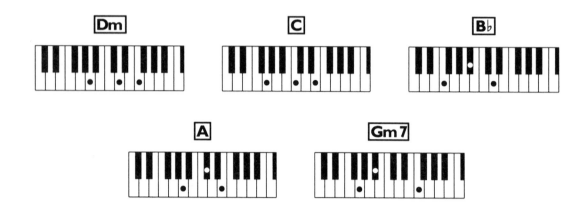

Voice:   **Brass 1**

Rhythm:   **Lambada**

Tempo:   ♩ = 104

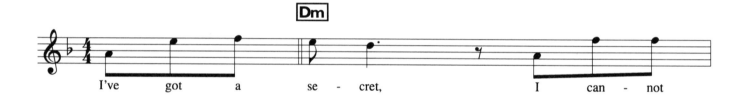

I've got a se - cret, I can - not

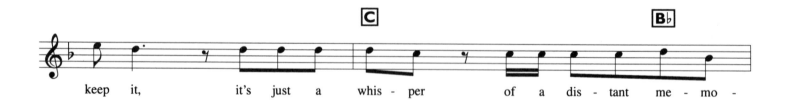

keep it, it's just a whis - per of a dis - tant me - mo -

- ry. Just a dream or so it

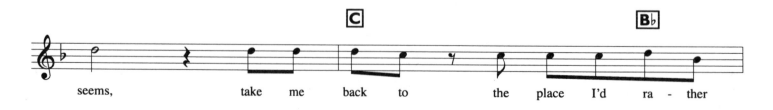

seems, take me back to the place I'd ra - ther

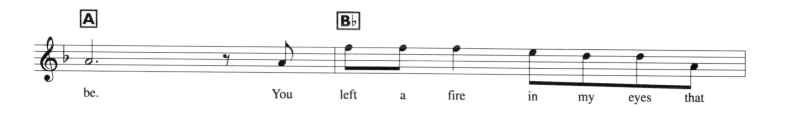

be. You left a fire in my eyes that

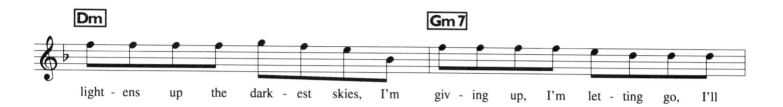

light - ens up the dark - est skies, I'm giv - ing up, I'm let - ting go, I'll

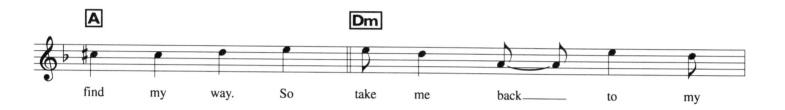

find my way. So take me back_____ to my

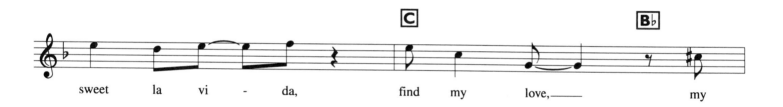

sweet la vi - da, find my love,_____ my

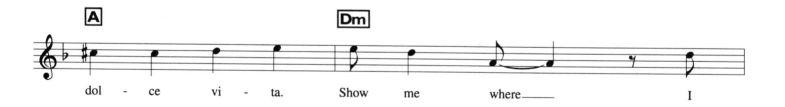

dol - ce vi - ta. Show me where_____ I

need to go,_____ don - de e - sta,_____ mi

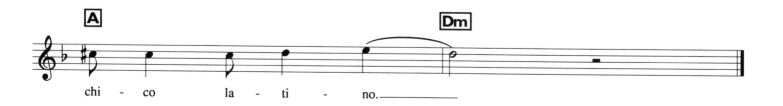

chi - co la - ti - no._____

# MISSING

**Words & Music by Tracey Thorn & Ben Watt**

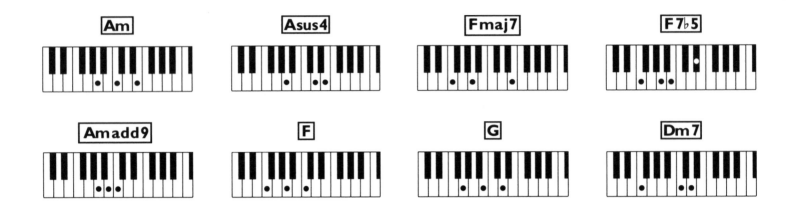

Voice: **Piano**

Rhythm: **Soft Rock 1**

Tempo: ♩ = **128**

I step off the train again. I'm walk-ing down your street

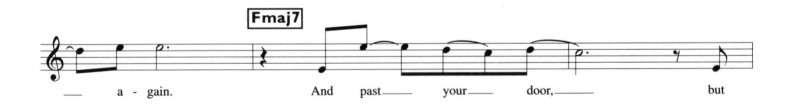

a - gain. And past your door, but

you don't live there a - ny-more. It's years since you've been there.

And now you've dis-ap-peared some -

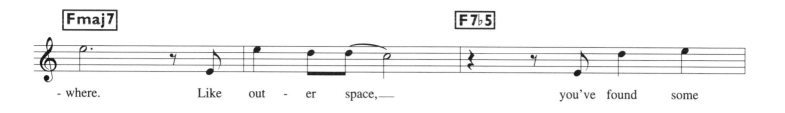

-where. Like out - er space, ___ you've found some

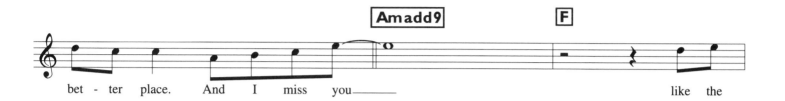

bet - ter place. And I miss you ___ like the

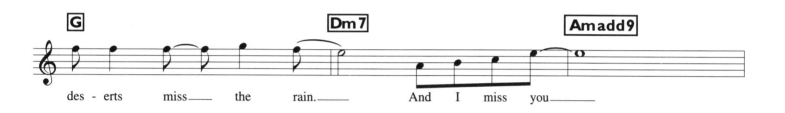

des - erts miss ___ the rain. ___ And I miss you ___

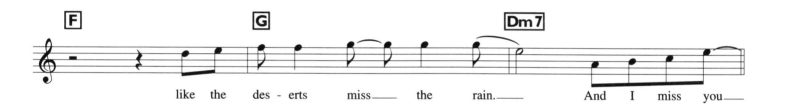

like the des - erts miss ___ the rain. ___ And I miss you ___

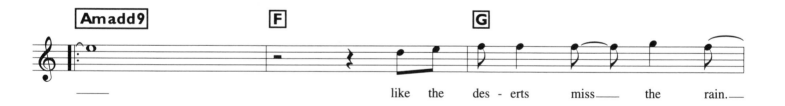

___ like the des - erts miss ___ the rain. ___

___ And I miss you ___ like the

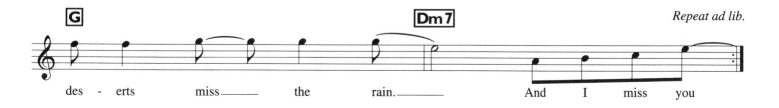

des - erts miss ___ the rain. ___ And I miss you

47

# MORE THAN A WOMAN

*Words & Music by Barry Gibb, Robin Gibb & Maurice Gibb*

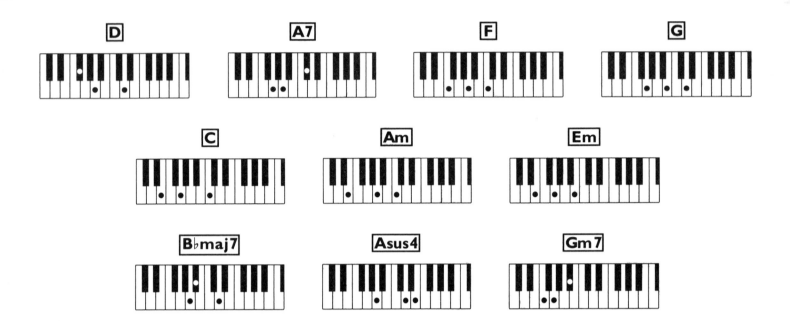

Voice: **Distortion Guitar**

Rhythm: **Techno**

Tempo: ♩ = 110

Girl, I've known you ve-ry well, I've seen you grow-ing ev-'ry day,— I

nev-er real-ly looked be-fore, but now you take— my breath a-way.

Sud-den-ly you're in my life, part of ev-'ry-thing I do. You've got me work-ing day and night, just

tryin' to keep a hold on you  here in your arms — I've found my pa - ra - dise, — my on-ly chance for hap-

- pi - ness, — and if I lose you now, I think I would die, — oh say you'll al-ways be my ba-by,

we can make it shine.  We can take for-ev-er just a mi-nute at a time, — oh. —

More than a wo - man,  more than a wo-man to me, — ba - by.

More than a wo - man, more — than a wo-man,  more than a wo-man to me. —

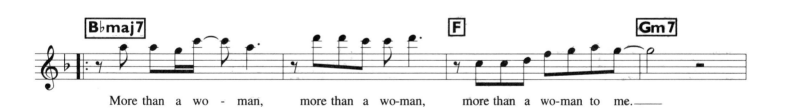

More than a wo - man,  more than a wo-man,  more than a wo-man to me. —

More than a wo - man,  more than a wo - man,  more than a wo-man to me, — ev-'ry day of my life. —

# NEVER EVER

**Words & Music by Shaznay Lewis, Esmail Jazayeri & Sean Mather**

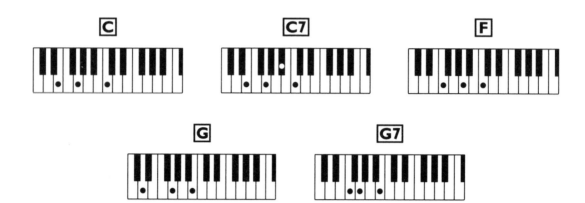

Voice:     **Saxophone**

Rhythm:    **16 beat**

Tempo:     ♩ = **72**

My head's spin - ning, ___ boy I'm in ___ a daze, ___ I feel i - so - lat - ed, ___

don't wan-na com-mu - ni - cate. ___ I'll take a show-er, I will ___ scour, ___ I will run ___

___ find peace of mind, ___ the hap-py mind, I once ___ owned ___ yeah. Flex-in' vo-cab-u-la-ry runs right through me.

The al-pha-bet runs right from A to Z. Con-ver-sa-tions, he - si - ta-tions in ___ my mind,

you got my con-science ask-ing ques-tions that I can't find. I'm not cra - zy. ___ I'm

# PERFECT MOMENT

***Words & Music by James Marr & Wendy Page***

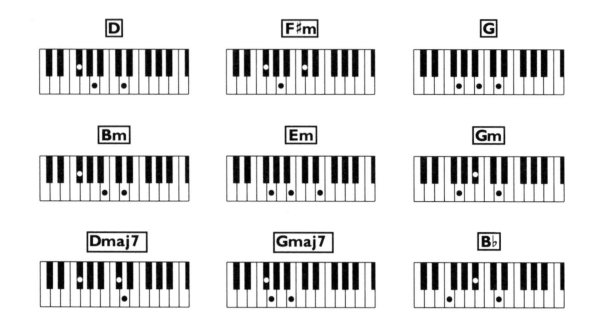

Voice: **Electric Guitar 2**

Rhythm: **Pop Ballad**

Tempo: ♩ = 68

This is my mo-ment, this is my per-fect mo-ment with you.

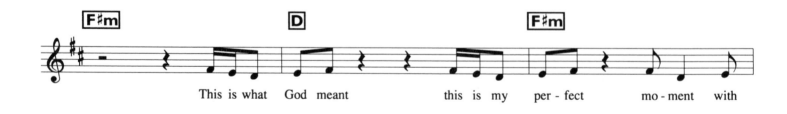

This is what God meant this is my per-fect mo-ment with

you. Wish I could freeze this space in

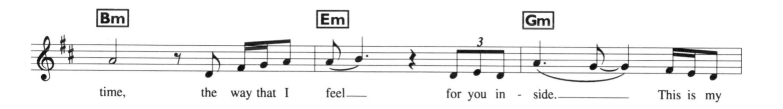

time, the way that I feel—— for you in - side.—— This is my

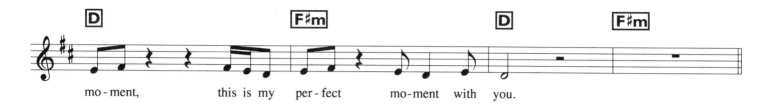

mo - ment, this is my per - fect mo - ment with you.

Tell me you love me, the mo - ment you leave, you're more than a sha - dow,

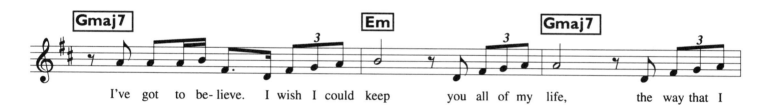

I've got to be - lieve. I wish I could keep you all of my life, the way that I

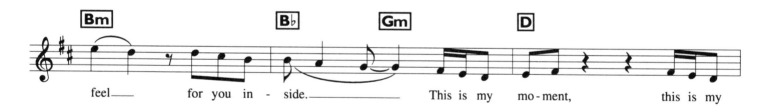

feel—— for you in - side.—— This is my mo - ment, this is my

per - fect mo - ment with you. This is my mo - ment,—— this is

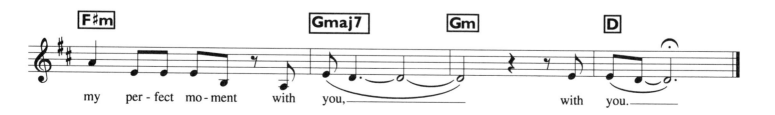

my per - fect mo - ment with you,—— with you.——

# ROAD RAGE

**Words & Music by Cerys Matthews, Mark Roberts,**
**Aled Richards, Paul Jones & Owen Powell**

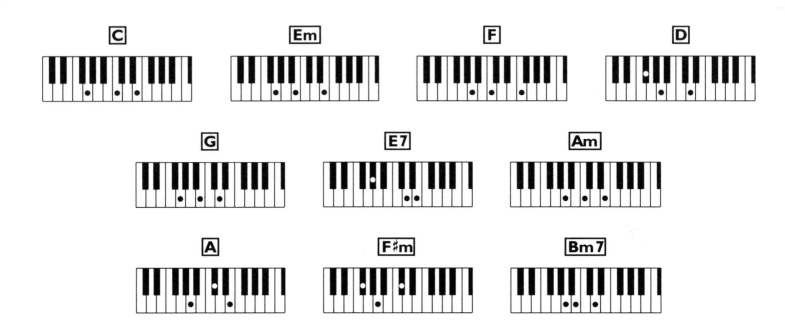

Voice:   **Distortion Guitar**

Rhythm:   **Soft Rock 1**

Tempo:   ♩ = 96

If all you've got to do to-day is find peace of mind,

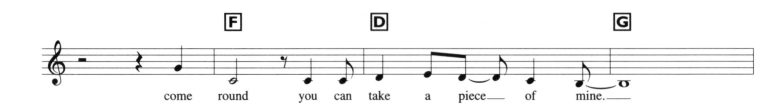

come round you can take a piece of mine.

And if all you've got to do to-day is he-si-tate,

come here,— you can leave it late— with me.

You could be tak-ing it ea - sy on——your-self, you should be mak-ing it ea - sy on—— your -

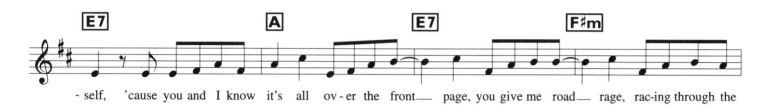

- self, 'cause you and I know it's all ov-er the front— page, you give me road— rage, rac-ing through the

best days. It's up to you— boy, you're driv-ing me cra - zy, think-ing you may - be los-ing your

mind. If all you've— got to prove— to - day— is your— in - no - cence,—

calm down, you're as guil - ty as— can be.

It's not ov - er, it's not ov - er, it's not ov - er.

# ROTTERDAM

**Words & Music by Paul Heaton & David Rotheray**

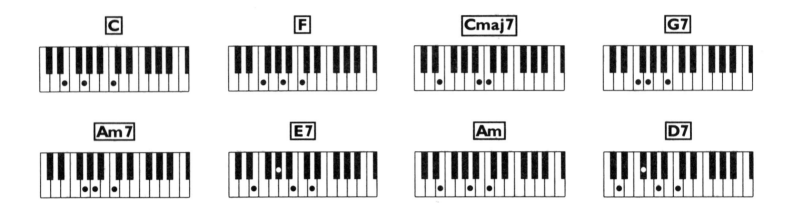

Voice: **Clarinet**

Rhythm: **2 beat**

Tempo: ♩ = 112

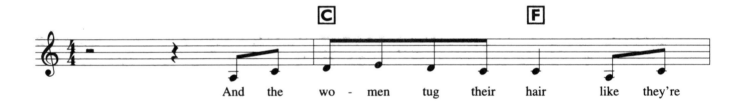

And the wo - men tug their hair like they're

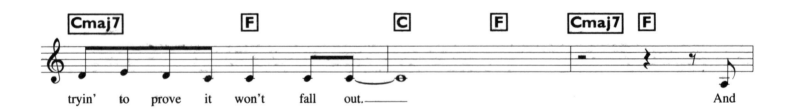

tryin' to prove it won't fall out._____ And

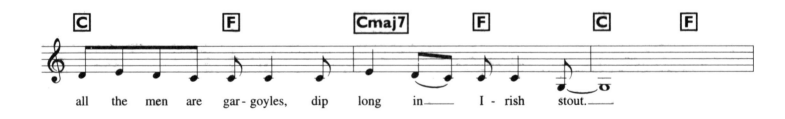

all the men are gar - goyles, dip long in___ I - rish stout._____

The whole place is pick-led, the peo - ple are pick - les for sure, and

no - one knows if they done more here than they ev - er would do in a jar.

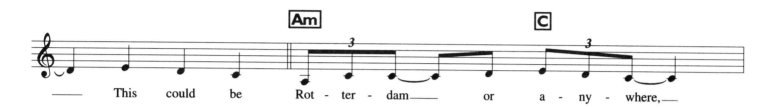

This could be Rot - ter - dam or a - ny - where,

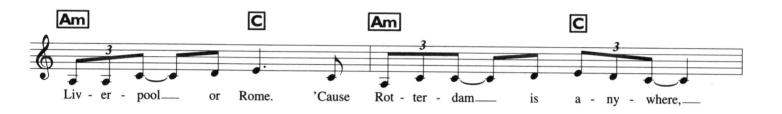

Liv - er - pool or Rome. 'Cause Rot - ter - dam is a - ny - where,

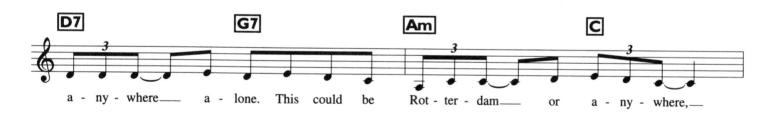

a - ny - where a - lone. This could be Rot - ter - dam or a - ny - where,

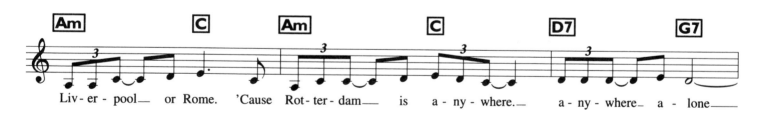

Liv - er - pool or Rome. 'Cause Rot - ter - dam is a - ny - where. a - ny - where a - lone

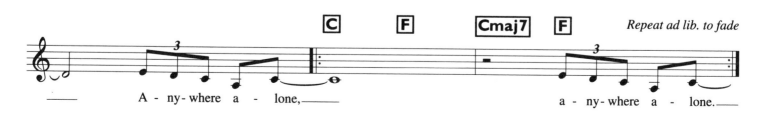

*Repeat ad lib. to fade*

A - ny - where a - lone, a - ny - where a - lone.

# SATURDAY NIGHT

***Words & Music by Alfredo Pignagnoli & Davide Riva***

Voice:     **Brass 2**

Rhythm:   **Twist**

Tempo:    ♩ = **130**

Sat - ur - day night____ I feel the air is get - ting hot,

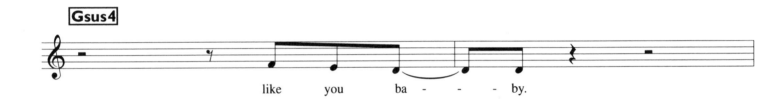

like you ba - - - by.

I'll make you mine,____ you know I'll take you to the top,

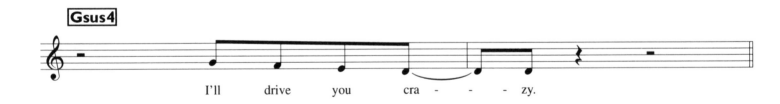

I'll drive you cra - - - zy.

Sa - tur - day night____ dance, I like the way you move.

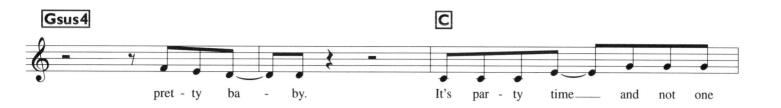

pret - ty ba - by. It's par - ty time___ and not one

min - ute we can lose, be my ba - by.

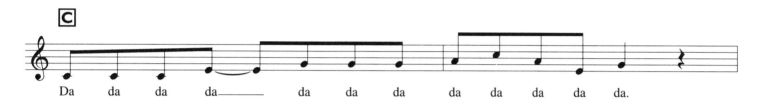

Da da da da___ da da da da da da da da.

Be my ba - by. Da da da da___ da da da

da da da da da. Pret - ty ba - by.

Da da da da___ da da da da da da da da.

*Repeat to fade*

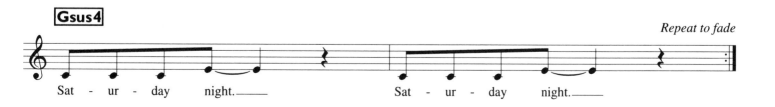

Sat - ur - day night.___ Sat - ur - day night.___

59

# SAY YOU'LL BE THERE

*Words & Music by Eliot Kennedy, Jon B, Victoria Aadams, Melanie Brown,*
*Emma Bunton, Melanie Chisholm & Geri Halliwell*

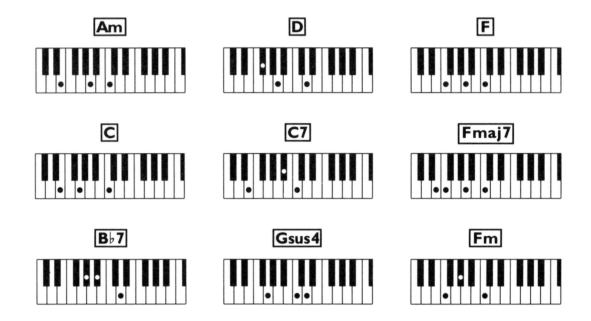

Voice: **Clarinet**

Rhythm: **Soul Ballad**

Tempo: ♩ = 108

Last time, that we had —— this con - ver - sa - tion,

I de - ci - ded we should be friends. —— But now we're

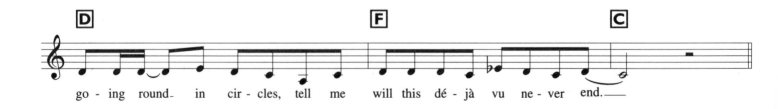

go - ing round — in cir - cles, tell me will this dé - jà vu ne - ver end. ——

Now you tell me that you've fall-en in love,___ well I ne-

-ver, ev-er thought that would be.___ This time you'

got-ta take__ it ea-sy, throw-ing far too much e-mo-tion at me,___ but a-ny fool

___ can see__ they're fall - ing, I got-ta make you un - der - stand.

___ I'm giv-ing you ev - ery - thing,__ all that joy__

__ can bring,__ this I swear.___ And all that I want

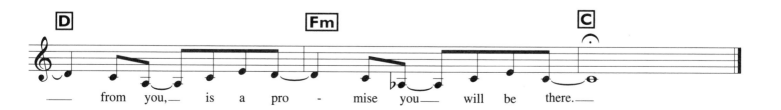

___ from you,__ is a pro - mise you__ will be there.___

# SEARCH FOR THE HERO

*Words & Music by Mike Pickering & Paul Heard*

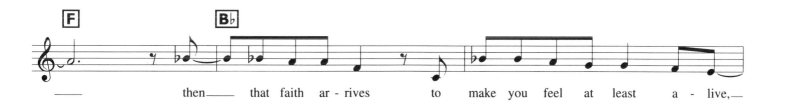

then that faith ar-rives to make you feel at least a-live,

and that's why you should keep on aim-ing high, just

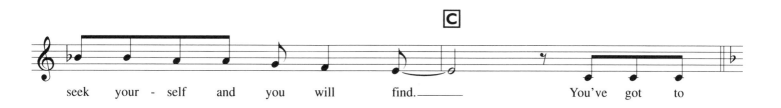

seek your-self and you will find. You've got to

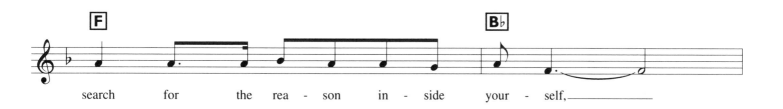

search for the rea-son in-side your-self,

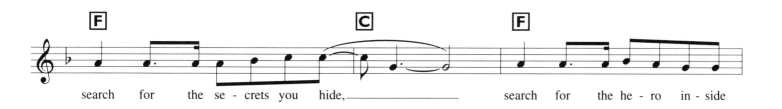

search for the se-crets you hide, search for the he-ro in-side

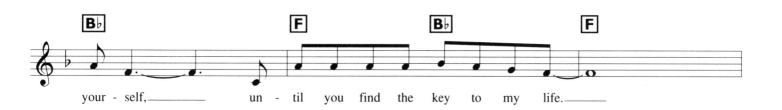

your-self, un-til you find the key to my life.

# SO YOUNG

**Words & Music by Andrea Corr, Caroline Corr, Sharon Corr & Jim Corr**

 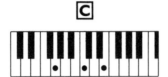 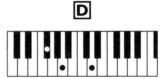 

Voice: **Violin**

Rhythm: **Folky Pop**

Tempo: ♩= 108

We were tak - ing it ea - - sy,

bright and bree - - zy,_____ yeah._____

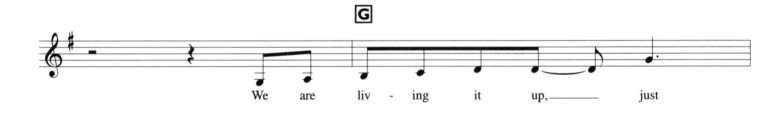

We are liv - ing it up,_____ just

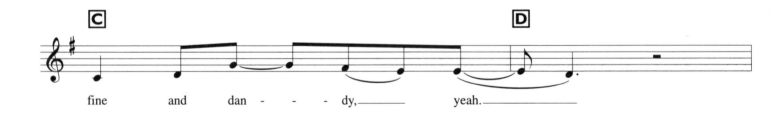

fine and dan - - dy,_____ yeah._____

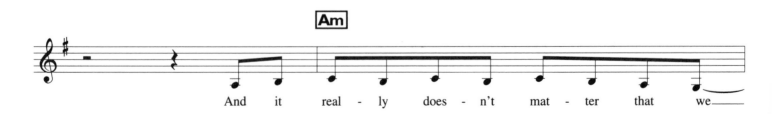

And it real - ly does - n't mat - ter that we

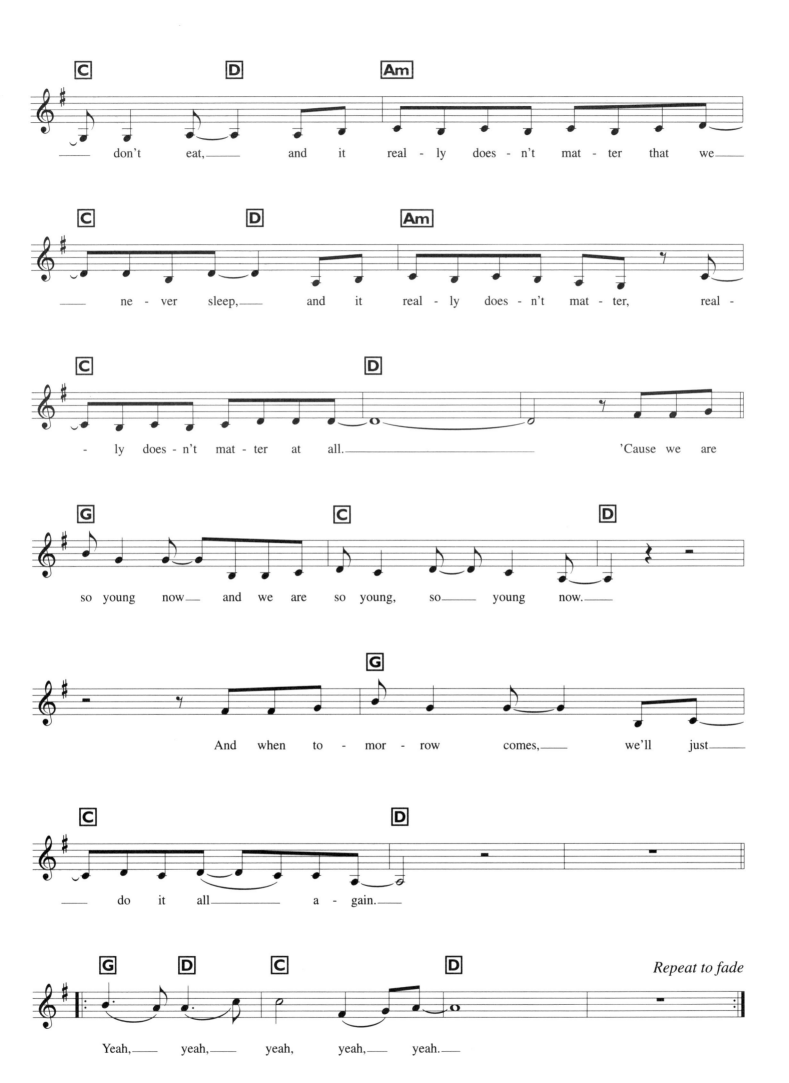

# STAY ANOTHER DAY

**Words & Music by Tony Mortimer, Robert Kean & Dominic Hawken**

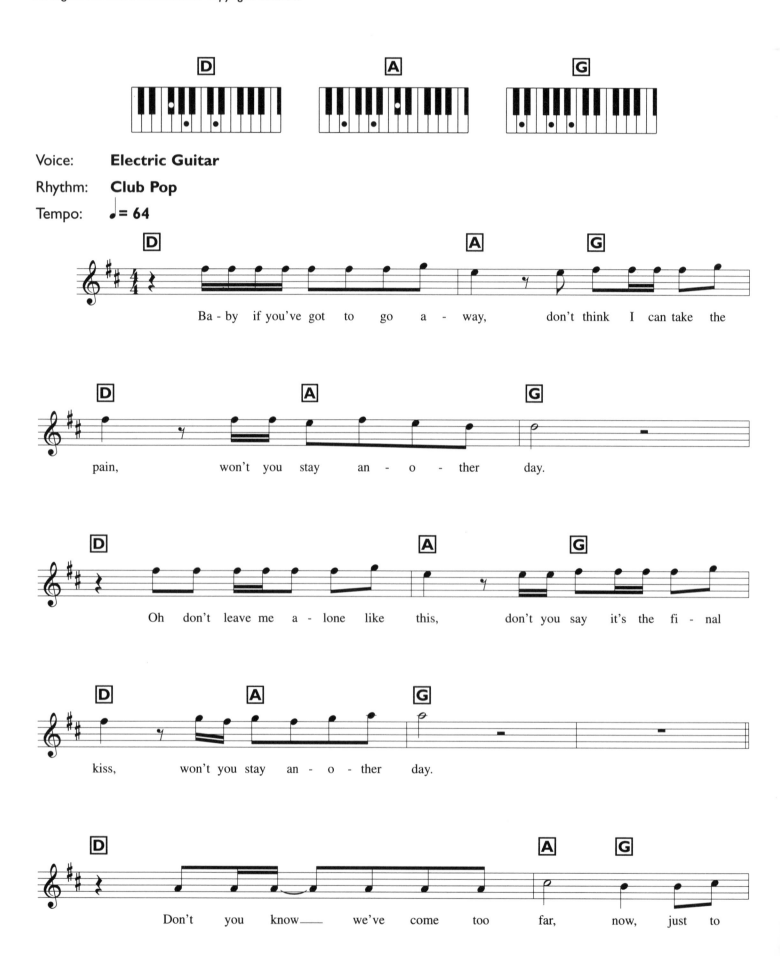

Voice: **Electric Guitar**

Rhythm: **Club Pop**

Tempo: ♩ = 64

Ba - by if you've got to go a - way, don't think I can take the

pain, won't you stay an - o - ther day.

Oh don't leave me a - lone like this, don't you say it's the fi - nal

kiss, won't you stay an - o - ther day.

Don't you know___ we've come too far, now, just to

go and try to throw it all — a - way. Thought I heard — you say you

love me, that your love was gon - na be here — to stay,

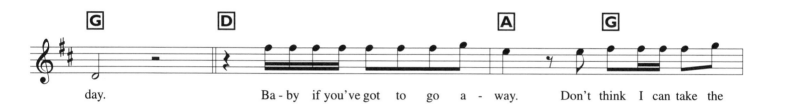

I've on - ly just be - gun to know you, all I can say is won't you stay just one more

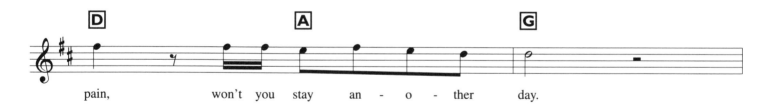

day. Ba - by if you've got to go a - way. Don't think I can take the

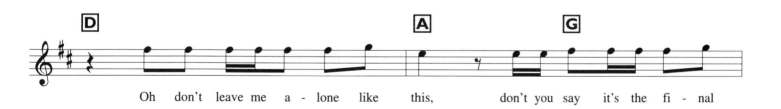

pain, won't you stay an - o - ther day.

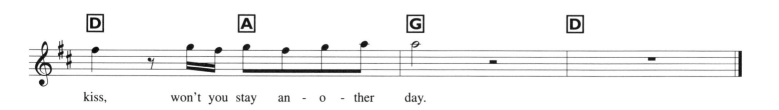

Oh don't leave me a - lone like this, don't you say it's the fi - nal

kiss, won't you stay an - o - ther day.

# THREE LIONS

*Words by David Baddiel & Frank Skinner*
*Music by Ian Broudie*

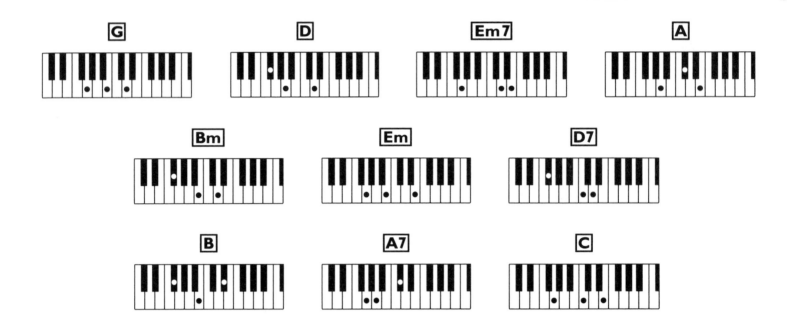

Voice: **Trumpet**

Rhythm: **Slow Rock (2)**

Tempo: ♩ = 126

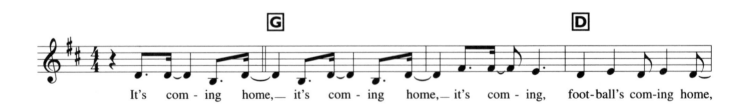

It's com-ing home,— it's com-ing home,— it's com-ing, foot-ball's com-ing home,

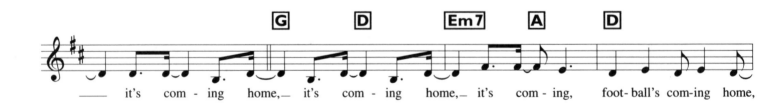

—— it's com-ing home,— it's com-ing home,— it's com-ing, foot-ball's com-ing home,

—— it's com-ing home,— it's com-ing home,— it's com-ing, foot-ball's com-ing home.—

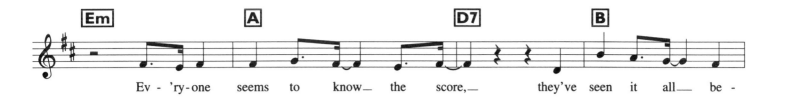

Ev - 'ry-one seems to know the score, they've seen it all be -

- fore, they just know, they're so sure that Eng-land's goin' to

throw it a - way, gon-na blow it a - way, but I know they can play 'cause I re-mem-ber

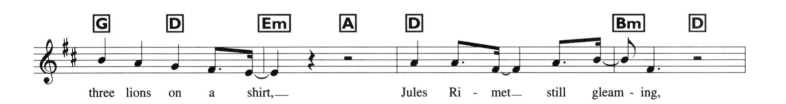

three lions on a shirt, Jules Ri - met still gleam - ing,

thir - ty years of hurt, nev - er stopped me dream - ing.

I know that was then but it could be a - gain.

It's com-ing home, it's com-ing, foot-ball's com-ing home. It's com-ing home,

# TORN

***Words & Music by Anne Preven, Scott Cutler & Phil Thornalley***
*© Copyright 1997 BMG Music Publishing Limited,*
*Bedford House, 69-79 Fulham High Street, London SW6 (33.33%), Weetie Pie Music &*
*Universal/Island Music Limited, 77 Fulham Palace Road, London W6 (33.34%) &*
*Scott Cutler Music/Screen Gems-EMI Music Limited, 127 Charing Cross Road, London WC2 (33.33%).*
*This arrangement © 1999 BMG Music Publishing Limited for their share of interest.*
*All Rights Reserved. International Copyright Secured.*

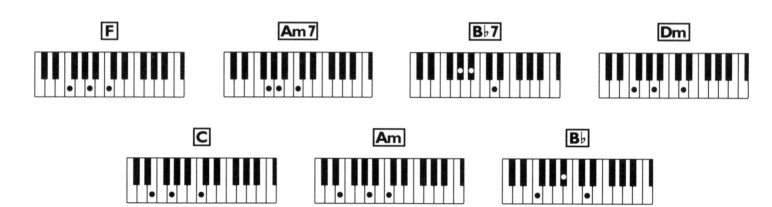

Voice: **Piano**

Rhythm: **16 beat**

Tempo: ♩ = **100**

I thought I saw— a man— brought— to life,—

he was warm, he came a-round— like he was dig - ni - fied,— he

showed me what it was— to cry.— Well you could-n't be— that man— I a-dored,—

you don't seem to know,— don't seem to care— what your heart is for.— But

I don't know— him a-ny-more,— there's no-thing where— he used to lie,—

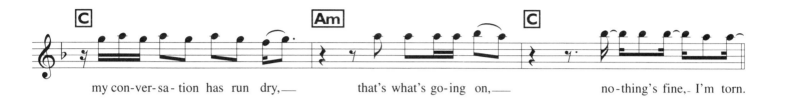

my con-ver-sa-tion has run dry,— that's what's go-ing on,— no-thing's fine,- I'm torn.

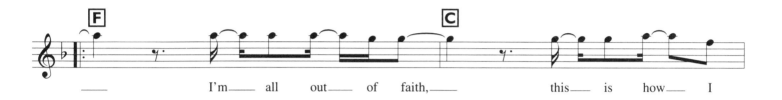

— I'm— all out— of faith,— this— is how— I

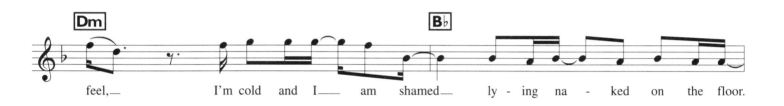

feel,— I'm cold and I— am shamed— ly-ing na-ked on the floor.

— Il-lu-sion nev-er changed— in-to some-thing real,— wide a-wake- and I—

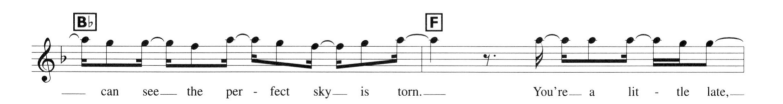

— can see— the per-fect sky— is torn.— You're a lit-tle late,—

*Repeat to fade*

— I'm— al-rea-dy torn.——— No-thing's right— I'm torn.—

# TURN BACK TIME

***Words & Music by Soren Rasted, Claus Norreen, Johnny Pederson & Karsten Delgado***
© Copyright 1997 MCA Music Scandinavia AB & Warner Chappell Music, Denmark.
Universal/MCA Music Limited, 77 Fulham Palace Road, London W6 (91.67%) &
Warner Chappell Music Limited, Griffin House, 161 Hammersmith Road, London W6 (8.33%).
All Rights Reserved. International Copyright Secured.

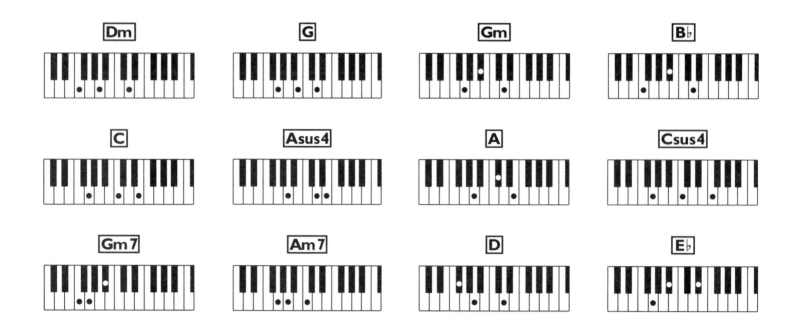

Voice:    **French Horn 2**

Rhythm:   **Lite Pop**

Tempo:    ♩ = 108

Give me time to rea - son,    give me   time   to think   it      through, —

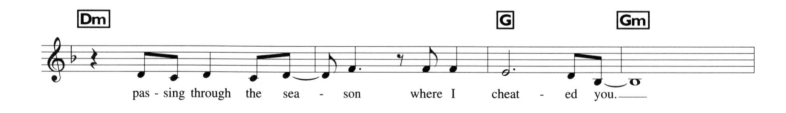

pas - sing through   the   sea - son   where I   cheat - ed   you. —

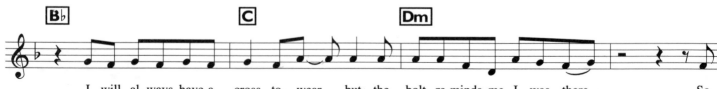

I will al-ways have a   cross to   wear — but the   bolt re-minds me I was there. —        So

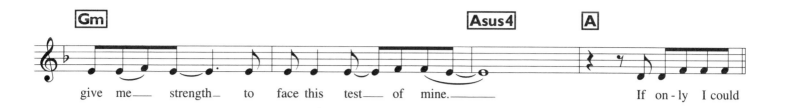

give me— strength— to face this test— of mine.———   If on-ly I could

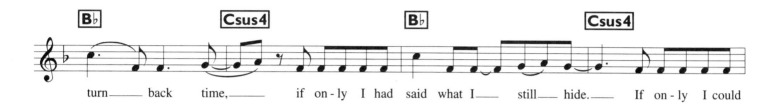

turn— back time,——   if on-ly I had said what I—— still— hide.——   If on-ly I could

turn— back time——   I would stay.

The nail re-minds me I was there.

The nail re-minds me I was there.   If on-ly I could

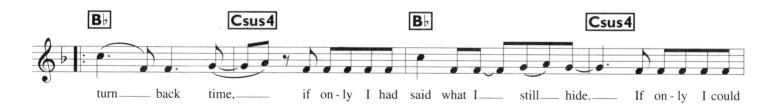

turn— back time,——   if on-ly I had said what I—— still— hide.——   If on-ly I could

*Repeat to fade*

turn— back time——   I would stay for the night.——   If on-ly I could

# 2 BECOME I

*Words & Music by Victoria Aadams, Melanie Brown, Emma Bunton,*
*Melanie Chisholm, Geri Halliwell, Matt Rowe & Richard Stannard*

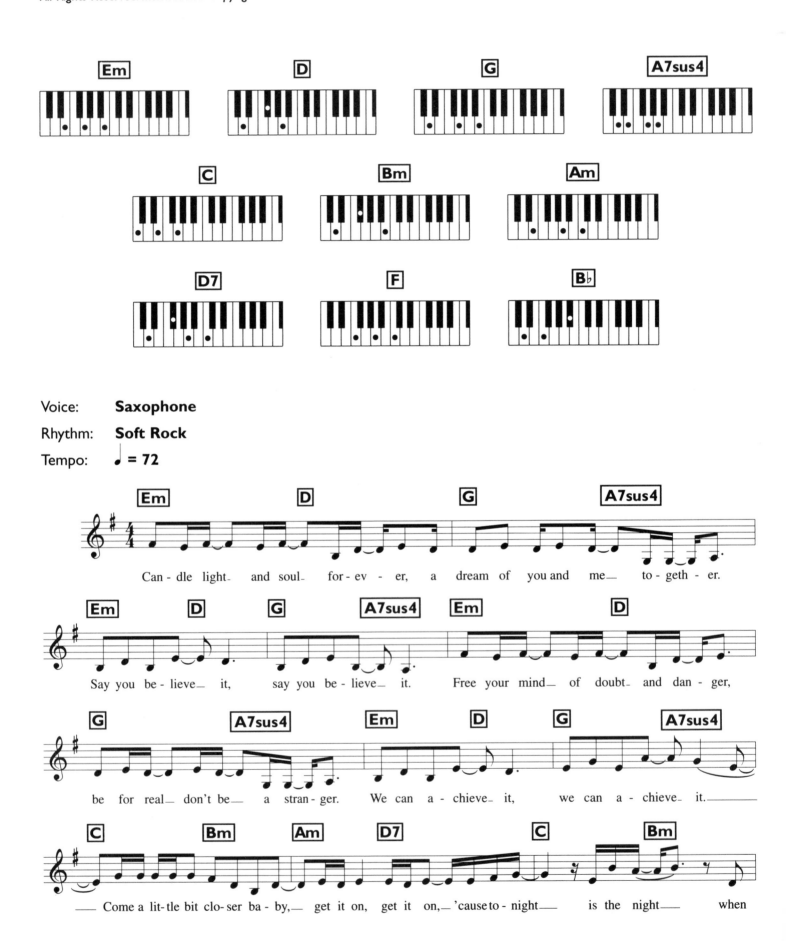

two be-come one.___ I need some love like I ne-ver need-ed love be - fore, (wan-na make love to ya ba-by.) I

had a lit-tle love now I'm back for more, (wanna make love to ya ba-by.) Set your spi-rit free,___ it's the

on - ly way to be.___

Be a lit-tle bit wi - ser ba - by,___

___ (put it on, put it on.)__ 'Cause to - night___ is the night___ when two be-come one.___ I

need some love like I ne-ver need-ed love be - fore,_(wanna make love to ya ba-by.) I had a lit-tle love, now I'm back for

more, (wan-na make love to ya ba-by.) I need some love like I ne-ver need-ed love be-fore,_(wan-na make love to ya ba-by.) I

had a lit-tle love, now I'm back for more,(wanna make love to ya ba-by.) Set your spi-rit free,_ it's the

*Repeat to fade*

on - ly way___ to be.___

It's the

75

# (UN, DOS, TRES) MARIA

**Words & Music by Ian Blake, Luis Gomez Escolar & Karl Porter**

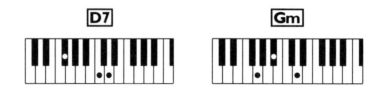

Voice: **Clarinet**

Rhythm: **Bossa Nova**

Tempo: ♩ = 132

She's the one— that al-ways turns me on, sex-y an-gel fall - ing from

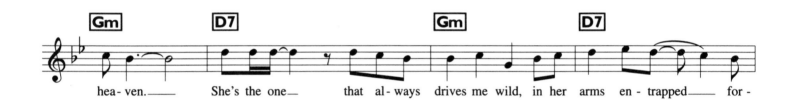

hea-ven.— She's the one— that al-ways drives me wild, in her arms en-trapped— for-

-ev-er. A-si es— Ma-ri-a blan-ca co-mo el di-a pe-ro es ve-

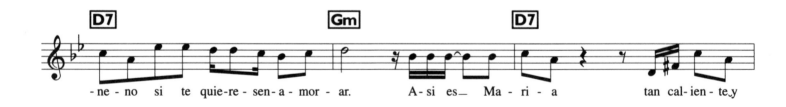

-ne-no si te quie-re-sen-a-mor-ar. A-si es— Ma-ri-a tan cal-ien-te y

fri-a que si te la be-bes, de se-gu-ro te va a ma-tar.—

Un dos tres, un — pa - si - to pa'de - lan - te Ma - ri - a. Un dos tres, un —

— pa - si - to pa' - tras. — Un dos tres, un — pa - si - to pa'de lan - te Ma- ri - a.

Un dos tres, un — pa - si - to pa' - tras. — Un —

— pa - si - to pa - lan - te, un — pa - si - to pa' - tras. — Un —

— pa - si - to pa - lan - te, un — pa - si - to pa' - tras. — Un —

— pa - si - to pa - lan - te, un — pa - si - to pa' - tras. — Un —

— pa - si - to pa - lan - te, un — pa - si - to pa' - tras. —

# WHAT CAN I DO

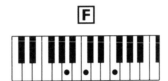
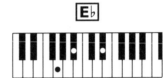

Voice: **Alto Saxophone**

Rhythm: **Folksy Pop**

Tempo: ♩ = 80

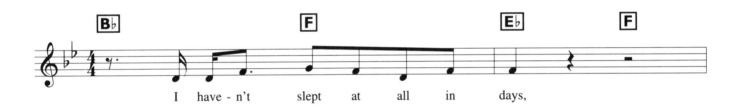

I have-n't slept at all in days,

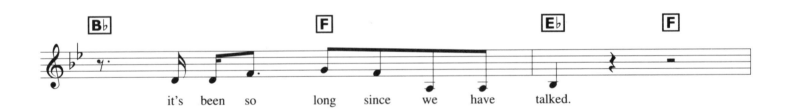

it's been so long since we have talked.

And I have been here ma-ny times,

I just don't know what I'm do-in' wrong.

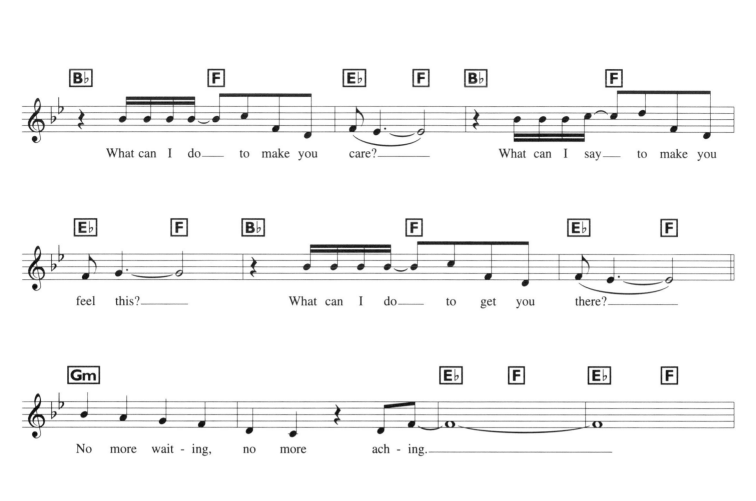

What can I do— to make you care? — What can I say— to make you

feel this?— What can I do— to get you there?—

No more wait - ing, no more ach - ing.—

No more fight - ing, no more try - ing.—

What can I do— to make you love me?—

What can I do— to make you care?— What can I say— to make you

*Repeat to fade*

feel this?— What can I do— to get you there?—

# WHEN YOU'RE GONE

*Words & Music by Bryan Adams & Eliot Kennedy*

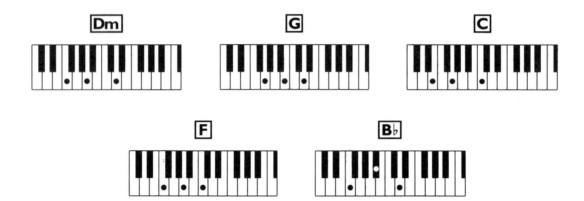

Voice: **Piano**

Rhythm: **Soft Rock 1**

Tempo: ♩ = 126

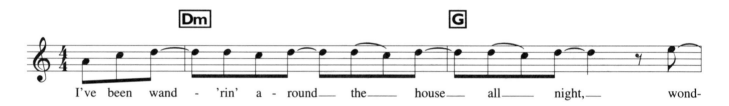

I've been wand-'rin' a-round the house all night, wond-

-'rin' what the hell to do. Yeah I'm tryin' to con-cen-trate but all

I can think of is you. Well the phone don't ring 'cause my friends

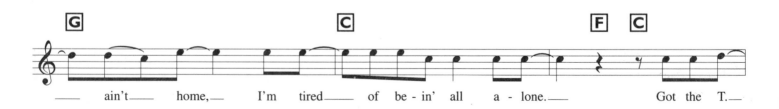

ain't home, I'm tired of be-in' all a-lone. Got the T.

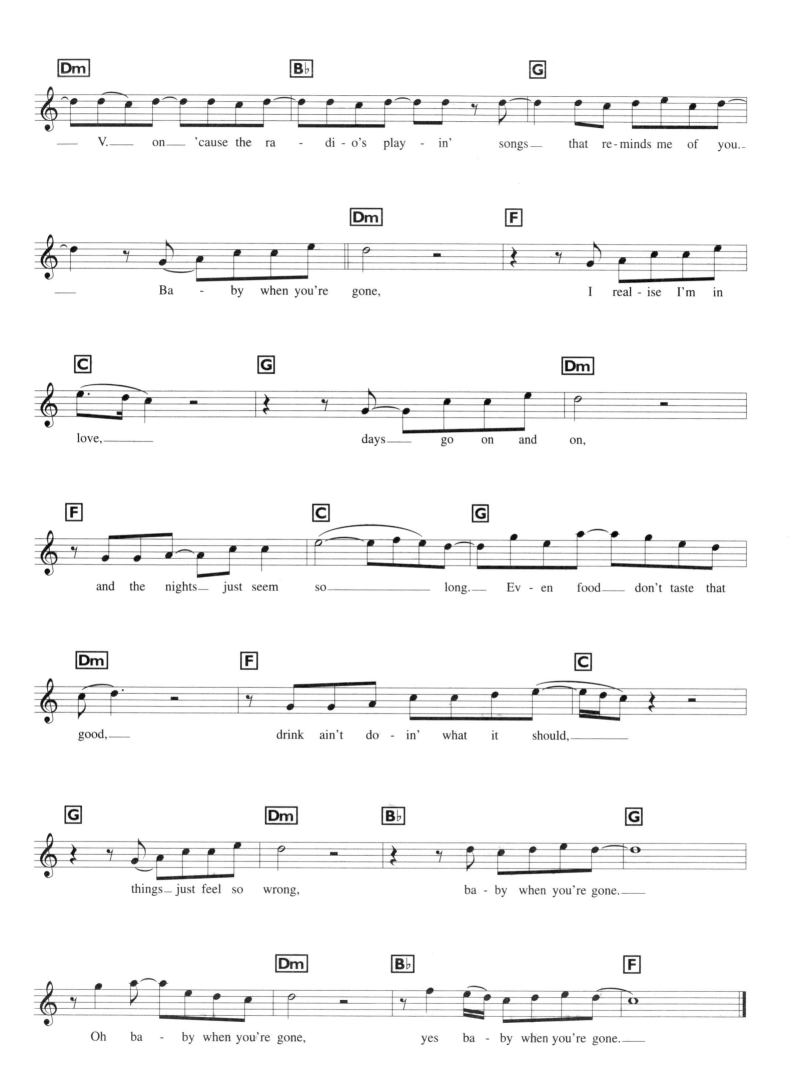

# WITHOUT YOU

**Words & Music by Pete Ham & Tom Evans**

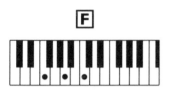
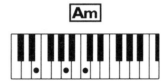
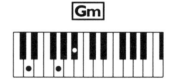
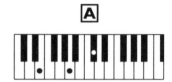

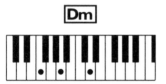

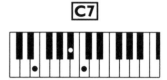

Voice: **Trumpet**

Rhythm: **Ballad**

Tempo: ♩ = 69

No I can't for-get this ev-'ning or your

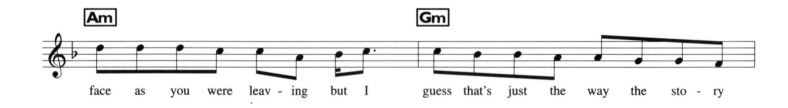

face as you were leav-ing but I guess that's just the way the sto-ry

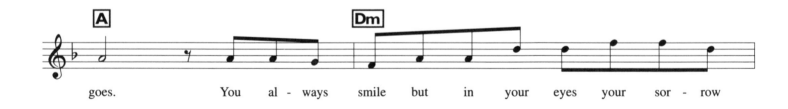

goes. You al-ways smile but in your eyes your sor-row

shows, yes it shows. No I

can't for-get to-mor-row, when I think of all my sor-row and I

had you there but then I let you go. And now it's on-ly fair that I should let you

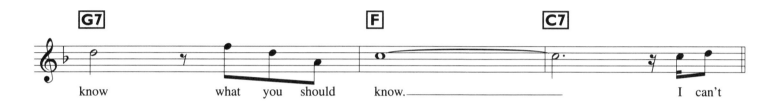

know what you should know. I can't

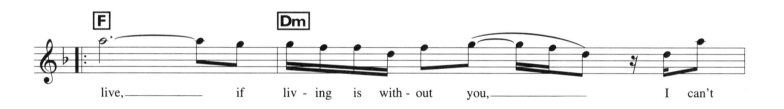

live, if liv-ing is with-out you, I can't

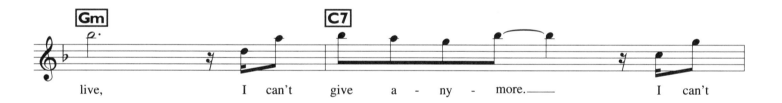

live, I can't give a - ny - more. I can't

live, if liv-ing is with-out you, I can't

give, I can't give a - ny - more. I can't

83

# WONDERFUL TONIGHT

*Words & Music by Eric Clapton*

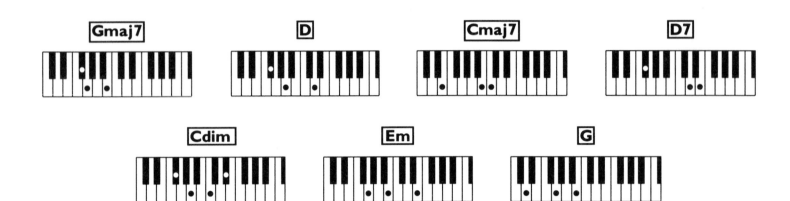

Voice: **Acoustic Guitar**

Rhythm: **Soft Rock**

Tempo: ♩ = 112

To - night, to - night,_____ to - night,_____

_____ to - night, to - night,— to - night,_____ to -

- night, to - night,— to - - - night.

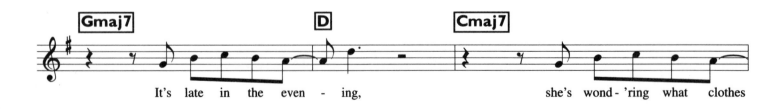

It's late in the even - ing, she's wond - 'ring what clothes

to wear, she puts on her make up

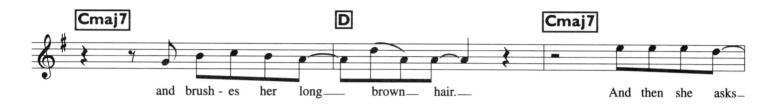

and brush-es her long brown hair. And then she asks

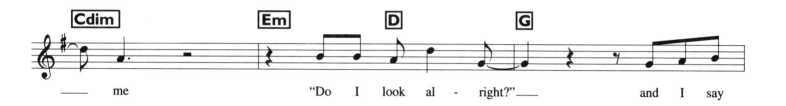

me "Do I look al - right?" and I say

"Yes, you look won - der - ful to - night."

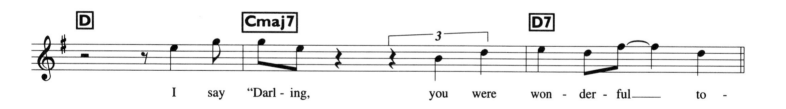

I say "Darl - ing, you were won - der - ful to -

-night." You look won - der - ful, you're ev - 'ry - thing I need and more.

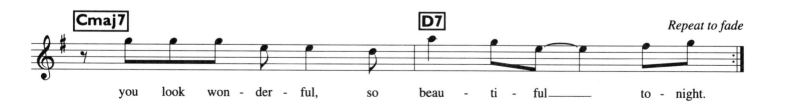

*Repeat to fade*

you look won - der - ful, so beau - ti - ful to - night.

# WONDERWALL

**Words & Music by Noel Gallagher**

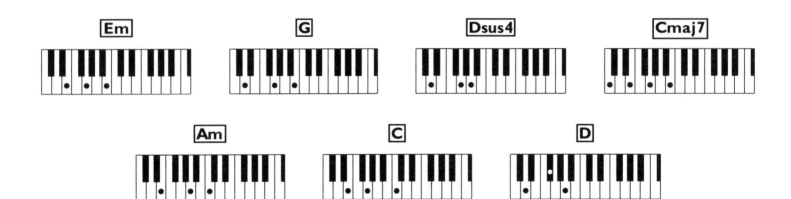

Voice: **Trumpet**

Rhythm: **Soft Rock**

Tempo: ♩ = 90

To - day    is gon - na be the day    that they're gon - na throw it back    to    you.—

By now you should've somehow re - a - lised what you got - ta    do.—    I don't be - lieve that  a - ny - bo - dy

feels    the way I    do—    a - bout    you    now.—

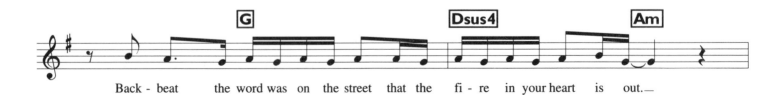

Back - beat    the word was on    the street    that the    fi - re    in your heart    is    out.—

I'm sure you've heard it all be-fore, but you ne-ver real-ly had a doubt.—

I don't be - lieve— that a - ny-bo-dy feels the way I do— a-bout you now.

———— And all— the roads— we have— to walk— are wind-

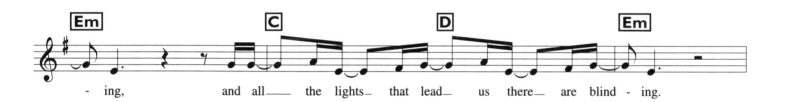
- ing, and all— the lights— that lead— us there— are blind - ing.

There are ma - ny things that I— would like to say to you,— but I don't know how.—

I said may - be,— you're gon - na be the one that

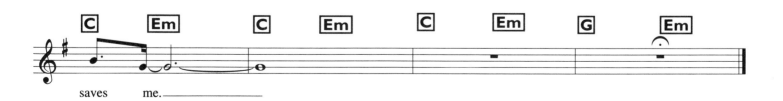
saves me.————

# WORDS

*Words & Music by Barry Gibb, Robin Gibb & Maurice Gibb*
© Copyright 1967 & 1975 Gibb Brothers Music.
*All Rights Reserved. International Copyright Secured.*

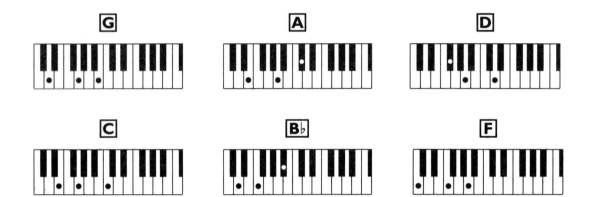

Voice: **Clarinet**

Rhythm: **Ballad**

Tempo: ♩ = 92

Smile an ev - er - last - ing

smile, a smile could bring you near to me. Don't

ev - er let me find you gone, 'cause that would bring a tear to me.

This world has lost it's glo - ry, let's start a brand new sto - ry

now, my love.      Right   now, there'll be no oth-er   time   and I can show you how,    my

love. ——        Talk   in ev-er-last-ing words   and de-di-cate them   all   to   me.

And   I   will give you all  my  life,   I'm here if you should call   to   me.

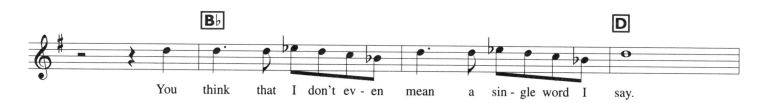

You   think   that  I don't ev-en   mean   a sin-gle word I   say.

It's on-ly   words,   and words are all  I   have   to take your heart a -  way.

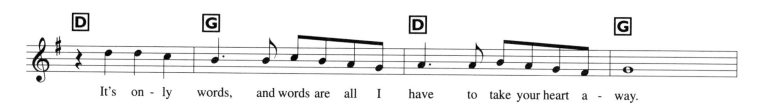

It's on-ly   words,   and words are all  I   have   to take your heart a -  way.

It's on-ly   words, and words are all  I   have   to take your heart a -  way.

# YOU GOTTA BE

**Words & Melody by Des'ree**
**Music by Ashley Ingram**

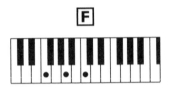
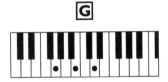
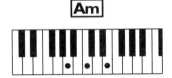
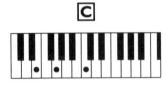

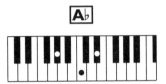

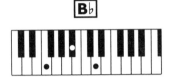

Voice: **Electric Piano**
Rhythm: **Pop Ballad**
Tempo: ♩ = 92

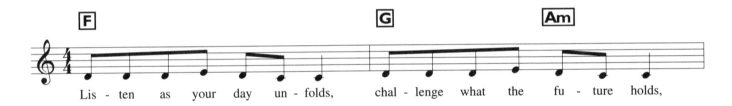

Lis-ten as your day un-folds, chal-lenge what the fu-ture holds,

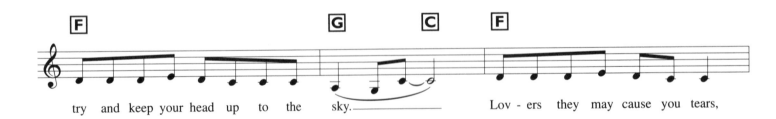

try and keep your head up to the sky.— Lov-ers they may cause you tears,

go a-head, re-lease your fears, stand up and be count-ed, don't be 'shamed to cry.— You got-ta be,

you got-ta be bad, you got-ta be bold, you got-ta be wis-er. You got-ta be hard, you got-ta be

# YOU MUST LOVE ME

**Words by Tim Rice**
**Music by Andrew Lloyd Webber**

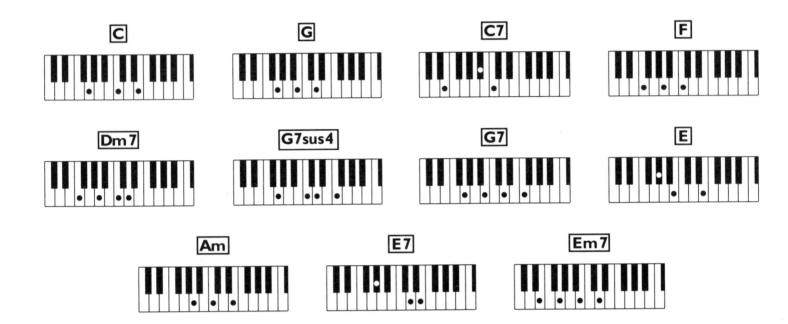

Voice: **Trumpet**

Rhythm: **Ballad**

Tempo: ♩ = 92

Where do we go from here? This is - n't where we in -

- ten - ded to be. We had it all, you be -

- lieved in me, I be - lieved in you.

Cer - tain - ties          dis - ap - pear,                    what do we do_____ for our

dream to sur - vive,          how do we keep____ all our pas - sions a - live          as

we used to do?_____                    Deep in my heart I'm con -

- ceal - ing          things that I'm long - ing to say,

scared to con - fess          what I'm feel - ing,          fright - ened you'll slip a -

- way.          You must love          me,                    you must love

me.                    You must love          me.

# YOU'RE STILL THE ONE

**Words & Music by Shania Twain & R.J. Lange**

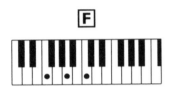 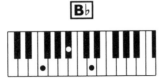 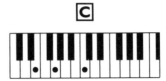 

Voice:     **Saxophone**

Rhythm:    **Soul Ballad**

Tempo:     ♩ = 138

Looks like we made it, look how far we've come

my ba - by. We might have took the long way,

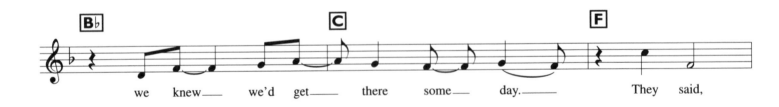

we knew we'd get there some day. They said,

I bet, they'll nev - er make it, but just

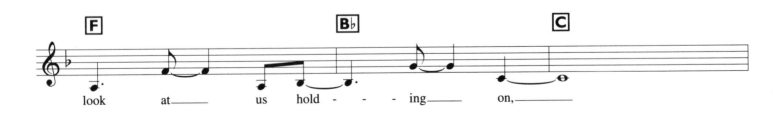

look at us hold - - ing on,

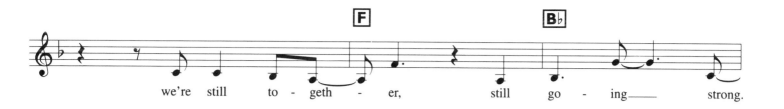

we're still to - geth - er, still go - ing____ strong.

____ (Still the one) You're still the one I run____ to,____

the one that I be - long____ to.____ You're still the one I want____ for

life. (Still the one) You're still the one that I____ love,____

the on - ly one I dream____ of.____ You're still the one I kiss____ good -

- night. I'm so glad we made____ it,____

look how far____ we've come my ba - by.____

# EASIEST KEYBOARD COLLECTION

Easy-to-play melody line arrangements for all keyboards with chord symbols and lyrics. Suggested registration, rhythm and tempo are included for each song together with keyboard diagrams showing left-hand chord voicings used.

 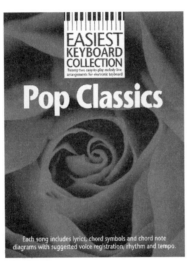  

## Showstoppers

Consider Yourself (Oliver!), Do You Hear The People Sing? (Les Misérables), I Know Him So Well (Chess), Maria (West Side Story), Smoke Gets In Your Eyes (Roberta) and 17 more big stage hits.
**Order No. AM944218**

## Pop Classics

A Whiter Shade Of Pale (Procol Harum), Bridge Over Troubled Water (Simon & Garfunkel), Crocodile Rock (Elton John) and 19 more classic hit songs, including Hey Jude (The Beatles), Imagine (John Lennon), and Massachusetts (The Bee Gees).
**Order No. AM944196**

## 90s Hits

Over 20 of the greatest hits of the 1990s, including Always (Bon Jovi), Fields Of Gold (Sting), Have I Told You Lately (Rod Stewart), One Sweet Day (Mariah Carey), Say You'll Be There (Spice Girls), and Wonderwall (Oasis).
**Order No. AM944229**

## Abba

A great collection of 22 Abba hit songs. Includes: Dancing Queen, Fernando, I Have A Dream, Mamma Mia, Super Trouper, Take A Chance On Me, Thank You For The Music, The Winner Takes It All, and Waterloo.
**Order No. AM959860**

## Also available...

**Ballads**, Order No. AM952116    **The Corrs**, Order No. AM959849
**The Beatles**, Order No. NO90686    **Elton John**, Order No. AM958320
**Boyzone**, Order No. AM958331    **Film Themes**, Order No. AM952050
**Broadway**, Order No. AM952127    **Hits of the 90s**, Order No. AM955780
**Celine Dion**, Order No. AM959850    **Jazz Classics**, Order No. AM952061
**Chart Hits**, Order No. AM952083    **Love Songs**, Order No. AM950708
**Christmas**, Order No. AM952105    **Pop Hits**, Order No. AM952072
**Classic Blues**, Order No. AM950697    **60s Hits**, Order No. AM955768
**Classics**, Order No. AM952094    **80s Hits**, Order No. AM955779

**...plus many more!**

# Mel Bay's
# SCHOOL OF
## Mandolin
# Irish Mandolin
by Joe Carr & Michael B. Gregory

GW00368034

## CD Track Listing

1 2 3 4 5 6 7 8 9 0
Clifford Essex Music Co. Ltd
7. Rose Walk, Wicken Green,
Fakenham, Norfolk, NR21 7QG.
Tel: 01485 529323. www.cliffordessex.net

# Contents

## Introduction

Welcome to *School of Mandolin - Irish Mandolin*! Here you will learn to play some of the most common Irish session tunes on the mandolin. If you love the Irish sounds of jigs, reels, and hornpipes played on the mandolin, this book is for you. You will also learn the basics of playing the mandolin for any style. We will study important Irish tune types (reels, jigs, etc) and some basic ornamentation. Intermediate and advanced players can learn new techniques and some great tunes! Let's get started and learn a little more about Irish style mandolin. For help learning to read tablature and standard notation, refer to *School of Mandolin MB21673BCD*.

## The Mandolin in Irish Music

While the mandolin has a relatively short history in Irish music, it is finding a place in the hands of great players such as Mick Moloney, Mary Shannon, Marla Fibish and others. Tuned in fifths just as the violin, all the standard Irish dance repetroire can be played on the mandolin. Most Irish music can be played in the first seven frets with no shifting required!

*Mandolins were being used occasionally in Ireland in the ceili bands of the 1930s, along with banjos, saxophones and other 'non-traditional' instruments. The type of mandolin being used was whatever was available at the time - the banjo mandolin was no doubt favoured for its volume, since electric amplification was more the exception than the rule in those days. The mandolin only really started to be taken seriously as a melody instrument in Irish Traditional Music in the late 1960s, partly due to the influence of bluegrass from America, partly riding on the back of the popularity of the Tenor Banjo (in no small part thanks to Barney McKenna of The Dubliners.)* --- David Eger June 2004 from Mandolin Cafe, discussion group

## How To Use This Book

This book can be used in several ways. The conventional approach is to simply read and play through the exercises and tunes using the CD for guidance. Alternatively, you could try the "by ear" approach traditionally used to learn and pass on Irish music. Using the clues given in the music, you can learn and memorize the tunes phrase by phrase. This approach is slow at first, but it will help you develop an essential skill for advancing Irish musicians - the ability to hear and repeat musical phrases. Also, you can combine the approaches. Learn some tunes by ear and others using the music. Listen repeatedly to the CD until you have the tune in your head. This helps memorization.

## Memorization

Irish music is played from memory. You will seldom, if ever, see Irish musicians playing in public using written music. The traditional way of learning Irish music is by ear. This is an important skill that can be developed. Strive to memorize each new tune by playing short phrases from the piece. Look for repeating phrases. In most tunes entire measures will appear more than once. It will get easier with practice.

## Accompaniment

Chordal accompaniment is a relatively new concept in Irish music and there are no standard chord changes to most tunes. Irish tunes are musically complete, containing all the required melody and rhythm when played by a solo instrument. The accompanist therefore has freedom to choose pleasant sounding chords. Listen to recorded examples for ideas.

## Irish Music Tune Types and Vocabulary

**Jig** – Jigs are typically written in 6/8 time and have a pulse of two beats per measure. The name "Flanigan" repeated over and over approximates the rhythm of a jig. *The Irish Washerwoman* is perhaps the most commonly recognized jig. Double jigs are usually simply called "jigs" and consist of two 8 measure parts which are each repeated resulting in a total of 32 mesures - AABB.

**Slide** – This member of the jig family is usually written in 12/8 time. Slides are most commonly found in the *Sliabh Luachra* area. The recurring "quarter note, eighth note" feel distinguishes slides.

**Reel** – Typically written in 2/4 or 4/4 time, reels are more like American fiddle tunes of any Irish tune type. Double reels are the most common consisting of two eight bar parts that are repeated twice in an AABB sequence to produce a 32 measure tune. Single reels are played ABAB resulting in a 16 bar tune.

**Hornpipe** - Played more slowly than reels, hornpipes are sometimes notated with dotted eighth notes to convey their typical bouncy feel. In many books, including this one, they are notated strictly with straight eighth notes for easier reading.

**Session** - An informal Irish music get-together. Sessions occur in pubs, clubs, restaurants and private homes. Typically, musicians sit in a circle, perhaps around a table, and perform sets of tunes from memory. Although some sessions may be held on a stage with sound equipment, it is more common that the instruments are unamplified. Sessions are generally for playing and listening rather than dancing.

**Set** - The tunes at a session are often played in sets of two, three or more tunes. Generally each tune in the set is of the same type and is usually played at least three times before moving (without stopping) to the next tune. Sets can be pre-arranged or they may be played spontaneously. Some sets are famous because of an important recording featuring an influential musician while others may become popular in a local area. Local sessions tend to develop their own familiar sets.

**Tune Names** - Irish tunes often have several names and good players may not even know the names of tunes they play! In this volume, common names and popular variants are given.

**Craic** - (pronounced *crack*) Irish word used often by musicians meaning good fun and company. It can also mean gossip.

**Ornamentation and Performance Notes** - Irish musicians vary a tune each time it is played. Through some melodic variation and varied ornaments, a tune is played differently every time. An advancing player should strive for this goal. The settings in this book are very basic versions.

**Note To Those With Bluegrass Experience**: Irish sessions differ from bluegrass jam sessions in that ALL the melody instruments are contributing EACH time through the tune. There is no soloing. Rhythm "chopping" is to be strictly avoided in Irish music.

## The Parts of The Mandolin

**Body** – The pear shaped or guitar shaped wooden part of the mandolin consisting of the top, sides and back.

**Neck** - The long wooden "arm" that extends from the body. The end near the body is called the *heel* while the flat part where the strings attach is called the *peghead*. Some necks have a hidden reinforcement rod for added strength.

**Peghead** - The flat piece of wood at the end of the neck away from the body. The tuning machines are attached to it and there may be a cover for the truss rod.

**Tailpiece** – The metal piece at the edge of the top where the strings attach. Some tailpieces have a cover which is removed by sliding the cover off the base of the tailpiece. Some tailpieces have 12 places to attach the strings. Before removing a string, study where it is attached and replace it exactly.

**Fingerboard** – This long flat piece of wood is glued to the top of the neck and holds the frets.

**Frets** - These pieces of wire are placed into the fingerboard. By pressing a string against the beaded top of these wires, melodies are played.

**Nut** – The strings rest on this plastic or bone piece that is glued on the peghead at the end of the fingerboard. The string slots in the nut should be adjusted so the strings are easy to push but not so low as to buzz. A repair person can easily make this adjustment.

**Tuning Machines** - Mandolin tuning machines are typically arranged 4 on a plate with four tuning buttons on each side of the peghead. These typically turn counterclockwise to raise the pitch on the upper side (G and D strings for right handers) and clockwise to raise pitch on the lower side (A and E.)

**Strings** – Mandolin strings come in sets of eight. The strings are numbered from highest in pitch to lowest so that the first string is the E string (closest to the floor when you are holding the mandolin). The typical mandolin set has four plain steel strings (E, A) and four wound ones (D, G.) The wound strings feature plain steel in the center wrapped with a much thinner bronze or steel wire. The strings have loops at the end. A ball end guitar string may be used on the mandolin in an emergency by carefully clipping the soft metal ball out of the loop using pliers or side nippers. Be careful not to snip the loop or it is useless!

**Bridge** – This is the wooden part which the strings cross after leaving the tailpiece. The bridge should not be glued in place. It is held in position by string tension only. The bridge position is very important and should not be moved. A misplaced bridge will cause the mandolin to play out of tune. If you suspect the bridge is not placed correctly, see a professional.

**Action** – This word describes the height of the strings above the fingerboard and the general playability of the mandolin. Adjustments to the string height at the nut and the bridge can make big changes in the ease of playing your mandolin. See a professional if you have questions.

**Changing Strings** - Remove and replace strings in pairs. If you remove all the strings at once, the bridge will fall off. If you have never changed strings on an instrument, it may be best to see a professional and ask to watch or look for detailed instructions on the Internet.

## Things To Check Before Starting

1. Is the bridge positioned properly? (See a professional)
2. Is the action good? (See a professional)
3. Are the frets in good shape? Loose, uneven or pitted frets can make playing difficult. (See a professional.)

## Holding The Mandolin

When sitting, the mandolin should be held comfortably in your lap with the neck elevated so the left hand can easily reach the neck. If you choose to use a strap, attach it while sitting and adjust it so that the mandolin remains in the same relative position sitting and standing.

## The Pick

Picks come in many styles and shapes, each with its own unique sound and feel. Experiment with them until you find one that suits you. A medium thickness, teardrop shaped pick such as a Fender Medium is a good place to start. The photograph shows the most popular pick grip.

## Hand Placement

Make a "V" with your left thumb and first finger. The mandolin neck should rest on the base of the first finger and slightly above the first knuckle of the thumb. There will be a small window of space between the neck and the bottom of the "V". (See photo.).Don't allow the neck to rest on the skin between your thumb and first finger. When stretching to play some high notes, you may have to slide the thumb towards the center of the back of the neck.

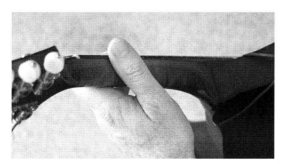

The right hand may rest lightly on the strings behind the bridge. Movement should come largely from the wrist. Another popular right-hand position involves resting the fourth and possibly ring finger of the right hand lightly on the finger rest (if your mandolin has one). You should strive to not plant or post these fingers as this will cause the wrist to be stiff or locked. Both positions are common and acceptable.

## Tuning

Good tuning is the easiest way to sound professional. The best player will sound awful if the mandolin is out of tune. Every time you play, check your tuning. Be sure to tune each pair of strings so that they sound the same (unison). There are several good methods.

1. Tuning Fork – An A 440 tuning fork will give you the note for the second string. Tap the fork on your knee and quickly place the ball end on the top of the bridge. Tune the second string to the resulting A note. See below *Tuning the Mandolin to Itself* for tuning the other strings.

2. Pitch Pipe – You may have a pitch pipe that plays each of the four notes: G, D, A, E (low to high.)

3. Electronic tuner – These are inexpensive and very accurate. Remember the names of the notes you are tuning. Most beginners, as well as more experienced players, prefer this device because it saves so much time.

4. Piano – If you have a piano or keyboard, the notes are: G below middle C (fourth string,) D above middle C (third string,) A above middle C (second string,) and E the second octave above middle C (first string.)

5. Guitar – If the guitar is in tune, play the third string (G) open for the fourth string G note. Play the guitar's second string (B) at the third fret for the second string D note. Play the guitar's first string at the fifth fret for the mandolin's second string A note. Finally, play the guitar's first string at the twelfth fret for the first string E note.

 1

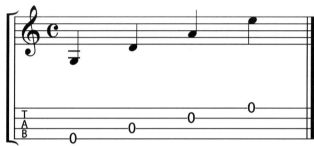

## Tuning The Mandolin To Itself

Sometimes you may want to tune the mandolin to itself or to another instrument. To do so, you can start with the first strings (E) or with the low fourth (G) strings. Since mandolin strings are in pairs, you should carefully tune each pair in unison so that you hear only one note when they are struck together.

A) Let's start with the G string (4).     2

1) Tune the G strings (4) to a note that sounds about right to your ear or to a G note from another source.
2) Fret the G strings (4) at the seventh fret for a D note.
3) Tune the open D strings (3) to this note. They should sound the same. (Unison)
4) Fret the D strings (3) at the seventh fret for an A note.
5) Tune the open A (2) strings to this note. They should sound the same. (Unison)
6) Fret the A strings (2) at the seventh fret for an E note.
7) Tune the open E (1) strings to this note. They should sound the same. (Unison)
8) Repeat the process listening for any inaccuracies. Pay special attention to each pair and make sure they are in tune.

B) Now let's start with the E string (1).     3

1) Begin with the in-tune E (1) strings.
2) Adjust the A strings (2) until the seventh fret E string note matches the open E (1) strings.
3) Play the open A (2) string and adjust the D strings (3) until the seventh fret A string note matches the open A (2) strings.
4) Play the open D (3) strings and adjust the G strings (4) until the seventh fret G strings note matches the open D (3) strings.
5) Repeat using method A, above.

## Fingering

Mandolin fingering is generally identical to violin fingering. Each finger is assigned two frets so that the first finger is used in frets 1 and 2, the second finger covers frets 3 and 4, the third finger 5 and 6 and the fourth finger plays fret 7. This may be modified as needed. Pay close attention to fingering so that you develop good habits from the beginning. Place your fingertips on the wooden fingerboard close to, but not touching the metal frets, listening for a clean note with no buzzing. Using close fingertip placement takes less effort to produce a good sound than placement towards the middle of the fret (between the metal frets.)

## Using The CD

Listen repeatedly to each new tune. If you can hum the tune before you start to learn it, you will have a much easier time. As you progress, you may even try learning a tune by ear from the CD, checking your accuracy against the music. This is the traditional way Irish music has been passed down through many generations.

## Pick Direction

Plectral or picked instruments are a relatively new addition to Irish traditional music (ITM.) As a result, there is no one correct way to pick this music. The pick directions given in this book represent good, solid, non-controversial techniques that will produce an Irish sound. Using the basic rules outlined below, beginners will have guidance when learning new melodies from tune books. Good habits built here will pay off down the road. Be aware that some great players ignore these rules completely while others may follow other logical (or ill-logical!) systems. Consider these rules as guidelines only. This being said, beginners and intermediates are advised to follow the pick directions in the book very closely. They have been worked out very carefully and with practice, will produce an authentic Irish sound. There are two basic patterns.

**Type: Alternating Picking**
Works in: Reels, Hornpipes, Polkas, – 2/4 and 4/4 time signatures.
The Idea: The down stroke is on the downbeat. A measure of 8 eighth notes begins with a down and alternates DUDUDUDU. A quarter note (on the beat) is played with a down stroke.
**Type: Jig Picking**
Works In: Jigs, Slides, – 6/8 and12/8 time signatures.
The Idea: Groups of three eighth notes are played DUD so that the down stroke remains on the strong downbeat of the music. Instead of alternating, the basic pattern is DUDDUD etc. When a quarter note is followed by an eighth note (for example, in a slide) the pattern is DU because the strong downbeat occurs on the quarter note.

## Let's Play!

We'll begin with *Oh Nelly, Nelly*, a polka in the key of D. Below is the D scale on the 3rd, 2nd and 1st strings. Notice the fret pattern on the 3rd and 2nd string is: 0,2,4,5. Practice playing this with all downstrokes. Repeat using alternating pick strokes.

 4

Here is the first two-measure phrase of *Oh Nelly, Nelly*. Begin by playing this with all down strokes. Memorize the phrase before moving on. This phrase will repeat. Count as you play these two measures. The first phrase could be said: "ONE and TWO AND ONE AND TWO AND." (Uppercase indicates picked notes while lower case indicates held notes).

 5

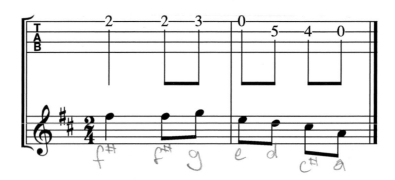

Notice the first measure of phrase 2 is the same as in phrase 1. The second measure is an answer to the musical question posed in phrase one. Memorize this phrase and then play the two phrases together without stopping. Say: "ONE and TWO AND ONE AND TWO and."

 6

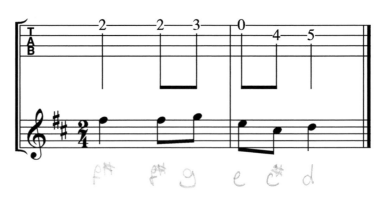

Phrase 3 is like phrase 1 with only one different note. Listen to the CD for the rhythm then play all three phrases together. We add the syllable ee to indicate the said rhythm: Say: "ONE and TWO AND ONE AND TWO and-EE".

 7

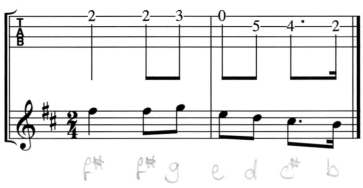

Phrase 4 is the ending phase that repeats in the B part of the tune. Memorize it and then play all four phrases together. The four phrases are called the A part. It is played twice before moving to the B part. Count: "ONE AND TWO AND ONE AND TWO and." Often in Irish music, the A part is referred to as the "tune" and the B part as the "turn."

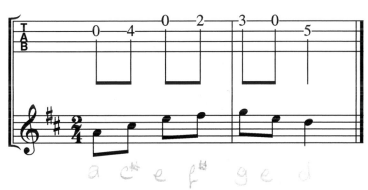

The B part (turn) begins with phase 5. Notice the measures are identical. Memorize this before moving on. Count: "ONE AND TWO AND ONE AND TWO AND."

Phrase 6 is just like phrase 4 except that it ends on a different note. Memorize as before and connect it. Count "ONE AND TWO AND ONE AND TWO and."

Phrase 7 is the last new phrase. It is like phrase 5 with an additional note and a different rhythm. Listen to the CD and memorize as before. Count: "ONE AND TWO-EE AND ONE AND TWO-EE AND."

Phrase 8 is the same as phrase 4. You now know the entire B part. Practice each part separately and then together. The entire tune appears on the next page.

**Reading Polka Rhythm** - Polkas have two pulses or beats per measure. Pat your foot along with the CD. The time signature of this tune is 2/4 meaning 2 beats per measure (the numerator of the fraction) and a quarter note (4) gets one beat (denominator). Two acceptable pick direction options are shown below. Option 1 (all down except for three notes) appears over the tab staff while option 2 (alternating) is above the music staff. Only upstroke symbols are given. All other notes are to be played with downstrokes.

 12

# Oh Nelly, Nelly

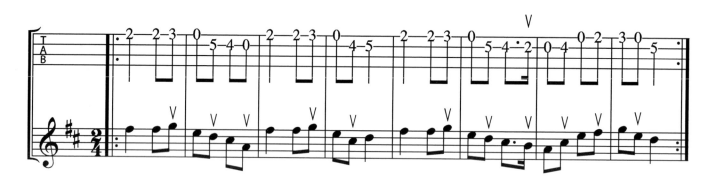

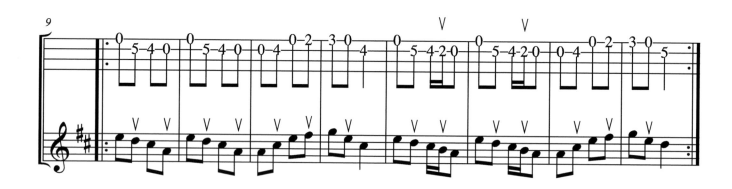

Our second tune is another polka in the key of A. Below is a one octave A scale. Notice it is like the D scale but moved over one string.

 13

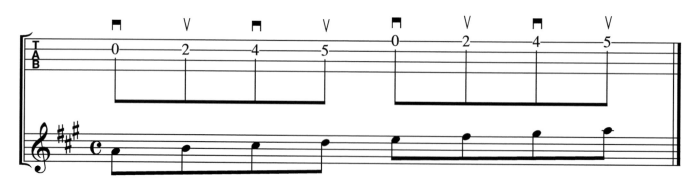

Listen repeatedly to this tune on the CD until you can hum it. Use the method we presented for *Oh Nelly, Nelly* and you will soon have the entire tune memorized. Notice measures 1 and 2 are the same as measures 5 and 6. Measures 3 and 4 are identical to measures 11 and 12. Measures 9 and 10 are the same as 13 and 14.

The rhythm of the first measure could be said thusly: ONE AND EE TWO AND. Measure two would be said: ONE AND TWO and. The quarter note (C#) lasts the entire second beat of the measure. Listen to the CD for help with this.

# I Have a Bonnet Trimmed in Blue

*Denis O'Keeffe's* is a slide. The characteristic slide rhythm is a recurring quarter note, eighth note pattern. The staff below contains the eight notes required to play this tune. Notice these notes only require the first and third fingers!

Using four beats we can count the rhythm: ONE ee AND TWO EE AND THREE ee AND FOUR ee AND.

 16

# Denis O'Keeffe's
### Denis O'Keeffe's Favourite
### Forget Your Troubles

Here is a tune Mike learned from the playing of John Brosnan - a Kerry box (accordion) player and repairman of high reputation. He called it a barndance, which is a tune-type very similar to a hornpipe. This tune is in the key of G. Pay attention to the new set of notes.

# The Keel Row

CD 17

**A Set of Jigs** - Spend time with the exercise on the next page before proceeding.

Now that you have four tunes memorized, (you do, don't you?) here are three jigs that can be played together as a set. Take time to master these tunes and don't become frustrated if your progress is slow. Learn each tune accurately by itself before moving to the next one. A slow, steady pace is preferable to fast and sloppy. Speed will come with time.

The first jig is *The Humours of Glendart*. "Humours" refers to the oddities or unusual aspects of the town, Glendart. Notice the first six measures use only the 1st and 2nd finger. Also note the identical measures in the A part: 1, 3, 5 and 2, 6. In the B part, measures 9-10 are identical to 13-14. Finally note that measures 15 and 16 of the B part are just like measures 7 and 8 in the A. Therefore, this 32 measure tune only has ten distinct measures!

Follow the indicated pick direction symbols very carefully. The DUD pattern shown here clearly defines the jig rhythm. Time spent here will pay off later. The 6/8 time signature means 6 eighth notes in a measure and an eighth note get one beat. There is one pulse for every group of three eighth notes resulting in two pulses (or foot taps) per measure. Listen to the CD.

# Jig Scale Exercise

Down-up-down pattern jig picking is an essential technique to achieve an authentic Irish sound. The exercises below should be practiced slowly giving careful attention to the pick direction symbols. As a dedicated student you will want to develop similar exercises for other keys. Work now will pay big benefits later. After some practice here move into the first jig set. The exercise uses a two-octave G scale.

 18

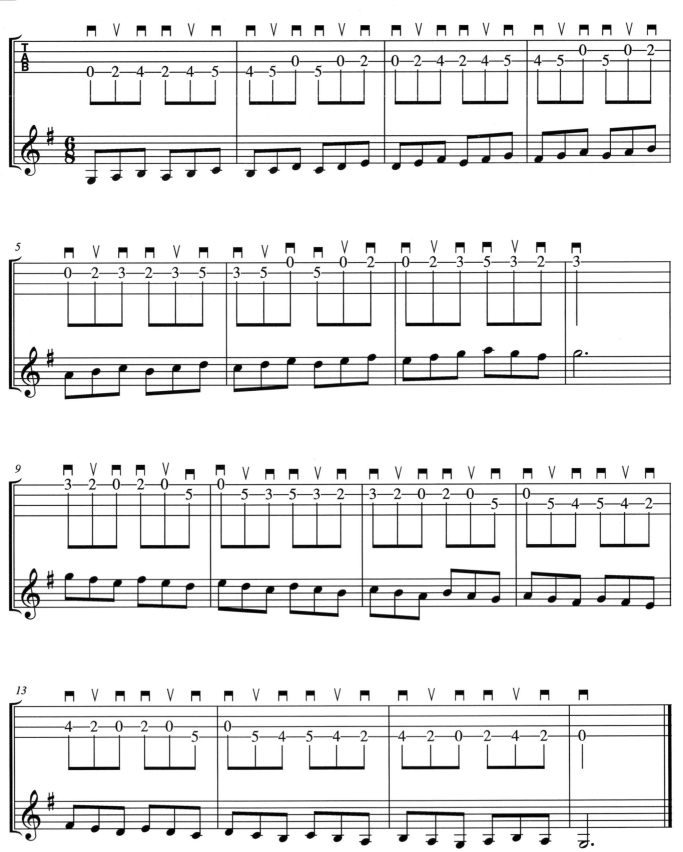

Jig Set 1 - Notice that the last note in measure 16 is the same A note as the very first note in the pickup measure. This A note should be played once when repeating the tune. When the tune is finished, the final note should be the first note of the next tune. In the case of *Out on the Ocean*, that note is also an A. If you end *Humours* without connecting it to another tune, the final note should be D (the next to last note in the measure.)

 19

# The Humours of Glendart
## The Cashel Jig

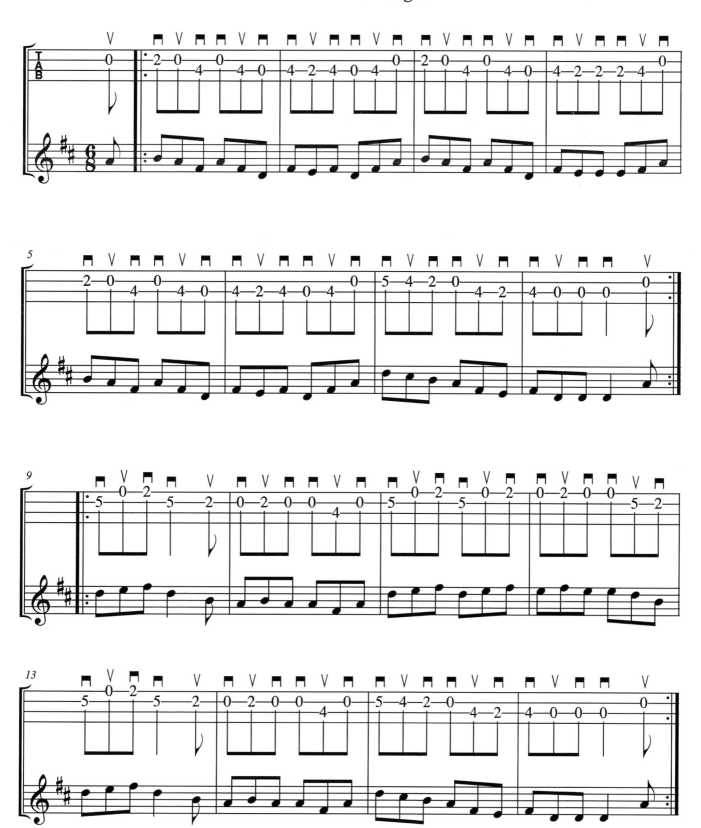

The second jig in this set is similar in some ways to *O'Keeffe's*. Although it is written in the key of G, the A part uses the same notes as the A of *O'Keeffe's*. It requires only the 1st and 3rd finger. Also notice identical measures: 2-6, 3-7-16 and 9-17. When you are ready to play the three jig set, play *Humours* three times followed directly by *Ocean* three times. Since *Tobin's* has no pickup note, lengthen the last G note to a dotted quarter.

# Out on the Ocean

 20

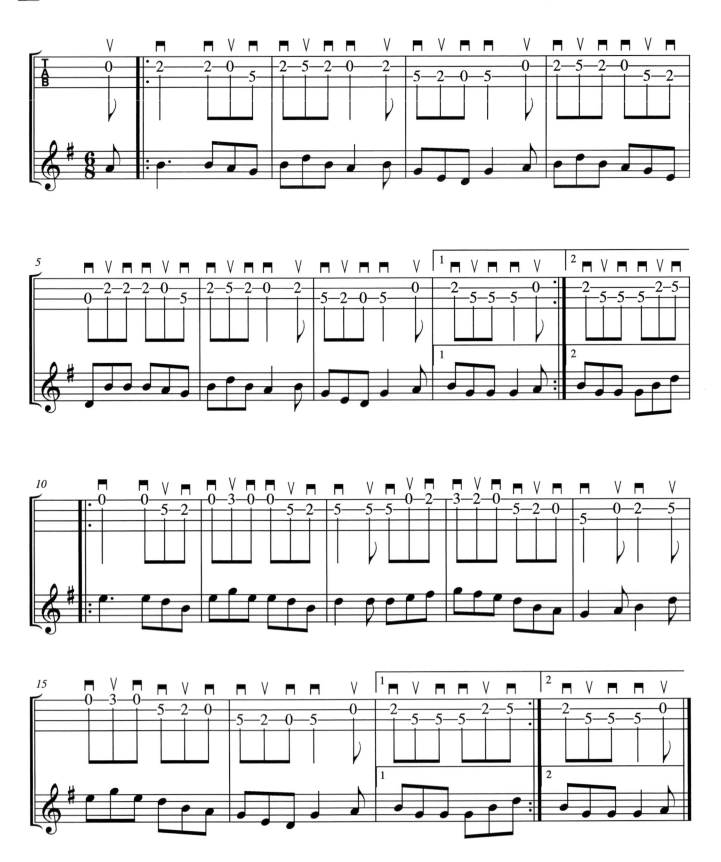

The third jig of the set has the most repetition of the three. Measures 1 and 2 are identical to 5 and 6 in the A part and 13 and 14 in the B part. Measures 3 and 4 are a phrase that repeats in measures 11 and 12. Finally measures 7 and 8 (the ending of part A) are repeated in measures 15 and 16. Play 3 times to complete the set. Learning a set of tunes and learning to move seamlessly from one to another is a skill that takes time and practice. Don't be discouraged - this will get easier with time.

 21

# Tobin's Favourite

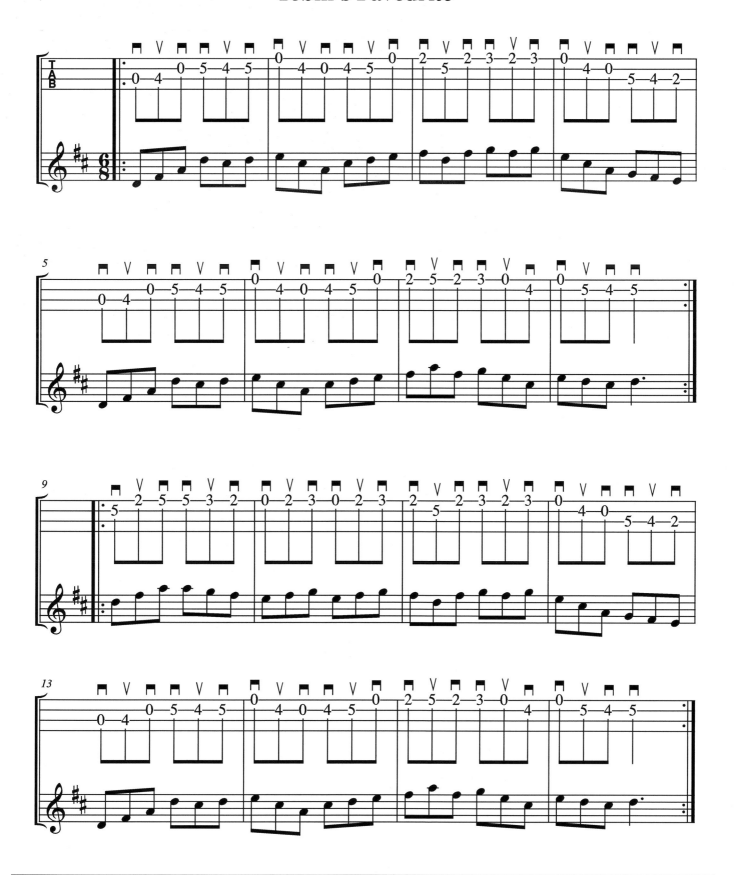

## Denis Murphy and Julia Clifford

Denis Murphy (1912-1974) and Julia Clifford (1914-1997) were sibling fiddlers from the Sliabh Luachra area. They were famous students of Pádraig O'Keeffe (1887-1963) - probably the most important and influential Munster fiddle player of the 20th Century. The 1968 recording *The Star Above the Garter* by Murphy and Clifford featured Kerry fiddle music and is considered a milestone.

 22

# Denis Murphy's Slide

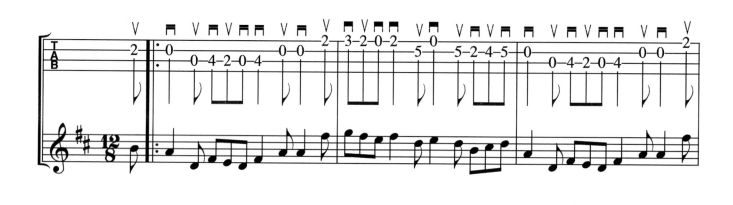

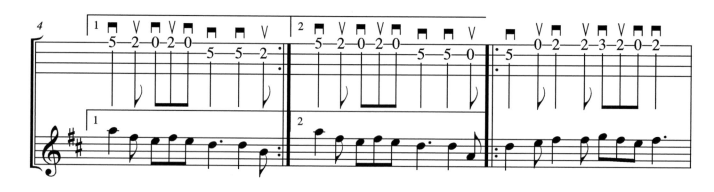

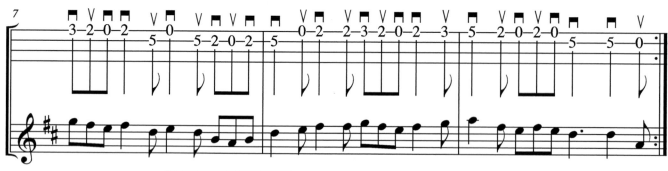

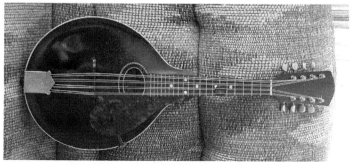

# The Star Above the Garter

**Jig Set 2** - In this set, we begin to use the fourth (pinkie) finger. The second tune has one B note at the seventh fret of the E string. Practice stretching the fourth finger to the seventh fret without moving your hand up the neck. Strive to reach seven frets comfortably from a single hand position.

**Jig Set 2** - Here is a two-jig set based on the Sliabh Luachra settings of box player Jackie Daly (on the CD *Street Life* by Patrick Street.) Notice that to move into *Boys of the Town*, you should play a G note (pickup note for *Boys*) rather than the B note at the end of the last measure.

 24

# Saddle the Pony
## The Red Stocking

**Jig Set 2 - Ornamentation** - In the second tune of our two-jig set, measures 3, 7 and 16 contain a very basic "doubled note" ornament. Ornamentation is used as a variation and is not played the same every time. Look for other places where you can play a similar kind of ornament. Memorize *Boys of the Town* and vary it slightly each time you play it. End the tune on the final lower G. In measure 9, the third finger plays a G followed by a D on the second string. Accomplish this by rolling the third finger from the third to the second string or by "hopping" the finger from string to string.

# Boys of the Town

**Hornpipe Set** - The first hornpipe is very well known in Irish music circles. Pay particular attention to the triplets in measures 2, 6 and 15. The two consecutive downstrokes between the D note on the 2nd string and the open 1st string E note deserve special attention. Spend time getting the pick direction and timing just right. Listen to the CD for help. Watch the fourth finger B note in measure 11. When moving to the next tune, substitute G and F# (from *Barley*) for F# and A.

 26

# The Boys of Bluehill

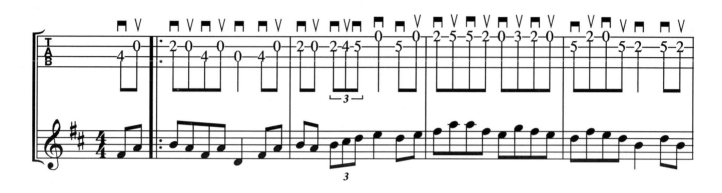

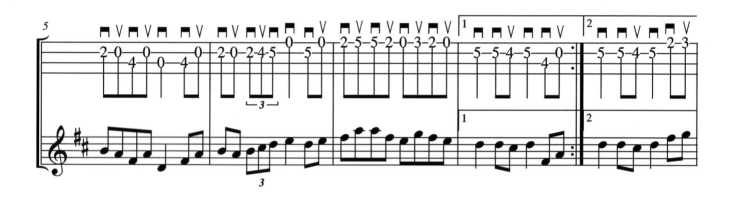

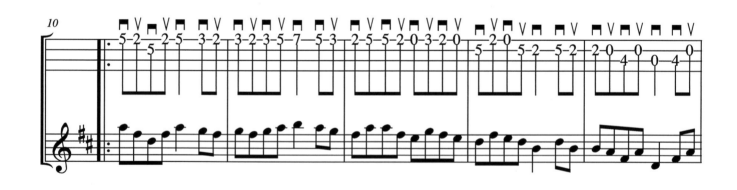

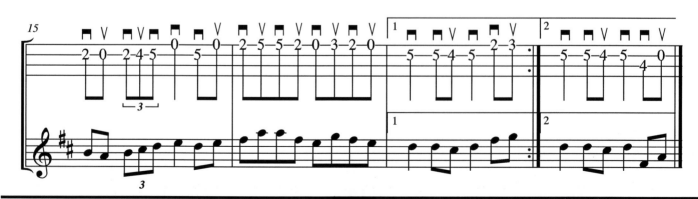

**Hornpipe Set** - The second hornpipe features repeated phrases in measures 1-2 and 5-6. Practice the triplet in measure 13 slowly at first, paying close attention to the pick direction. To connect to the final tune of the set, use the first two pickup notes of *Bantry* (G and A) instead of the G and F# in the last measure below.

 27

# The Stack of Barley

**Hornpipe Set** - In this final hornpipe of the set, notice the ending measures of the A and B part. Measures 7-9 are similar to measures 16-18.

 28

# Bantry Bay

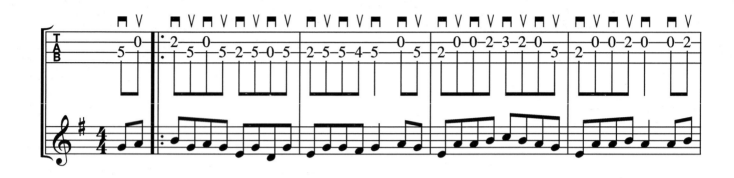

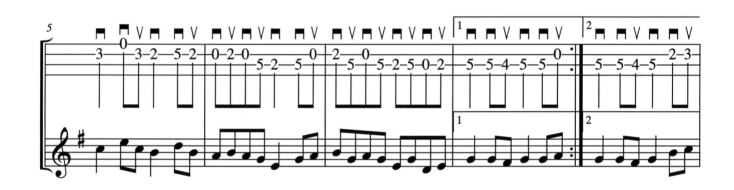

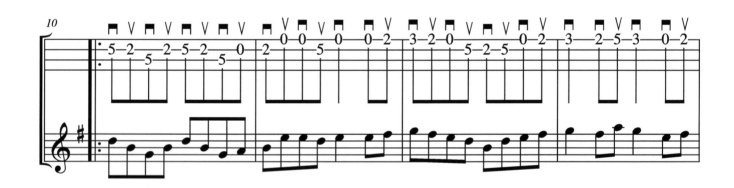

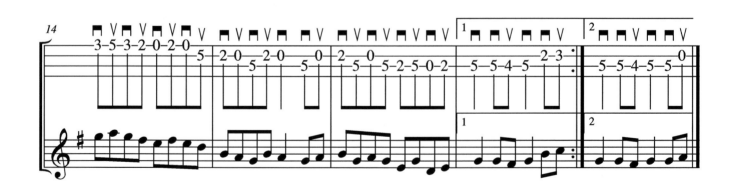

**Reel Set 1 - Tune 1** - Reels are by far the most popular tune type among Irish musicians. In a typical session, they represent half or more of the tunes played. Reels typically feature alternating picking so watch the symbols carefully. Measure 1 is like measure 5, measure 4 is like measure 8. Also note that measures 9, 11 and 13 are the same as are measures 10 and 14.

 29

# Lady Anne Montgomery

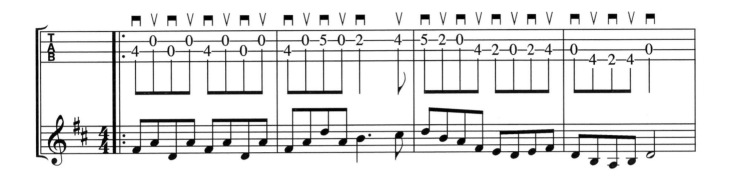

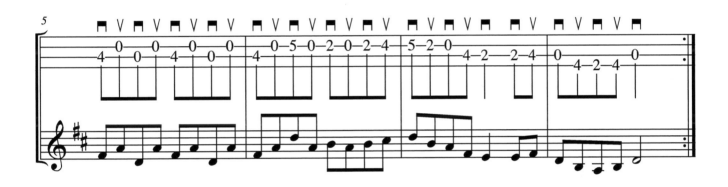

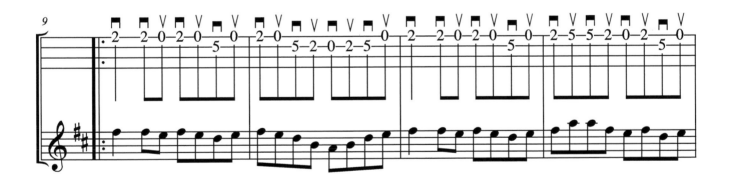

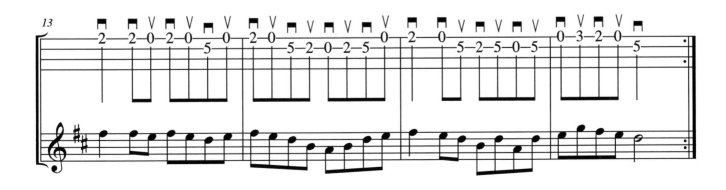

**Reel Set 1 - Tune 2** - The second reel is very popular. Notice that measures 1-2 repeat in 5-6. Also 7-8 and 15-16 match as well as 10-11 and 14-15.

30

# The Merry Blacksmith

**Reel Set 2 - Tune 1** - The third reel uses the fourth finger in measures 10, 12 and 14. Notice that measures 1-2 repeat in 5-6. Also 7-8 and 15-16 match as well as 10-11 and 14-15.

 31

# The Silver Spear

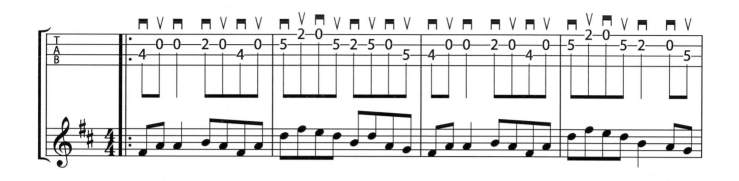

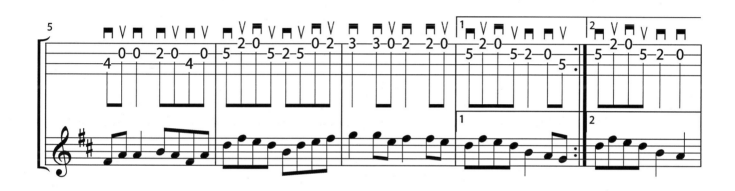

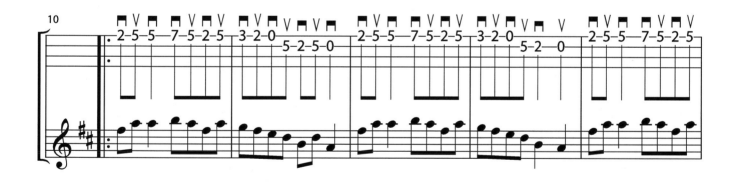

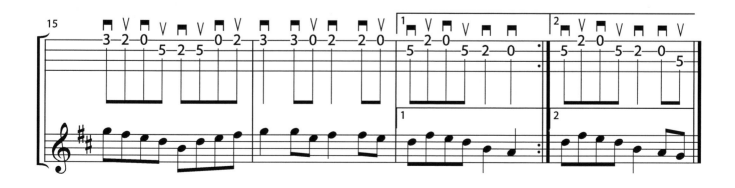

# Father Kelly's Reel

 32

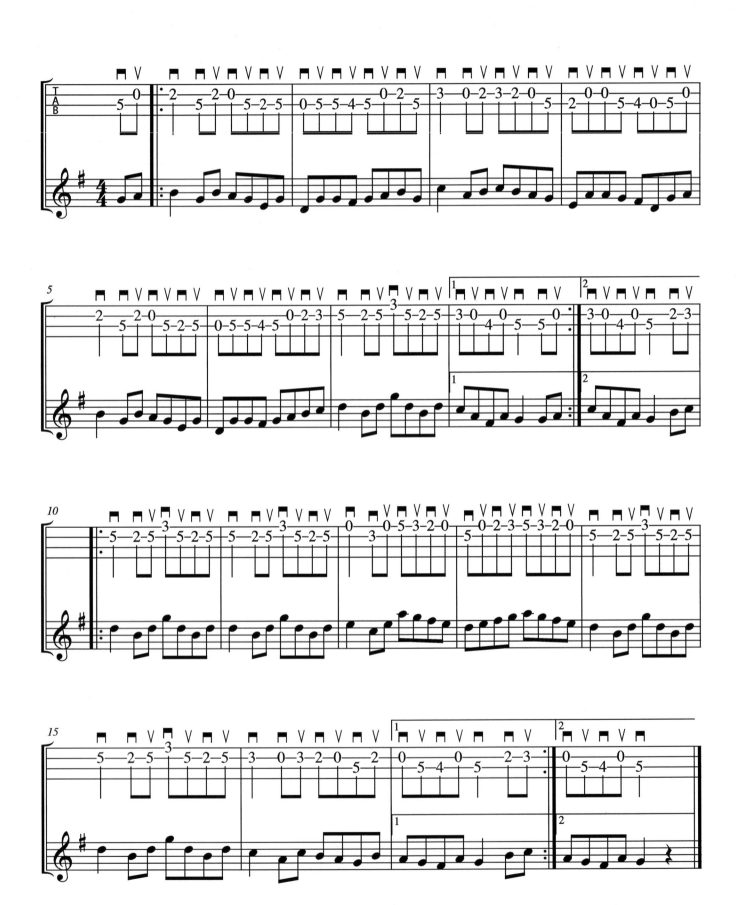

33

# Miss Monaghan

**Reel Set 3 - Tune 1** Measures 1 and 5 provide more practice with the first-finger roll. Place the first finger on the third string and roll to the second string or place the first finger tip so that it frets the single inside A and E string that are next to each other.

 34

## Cooley's Reel

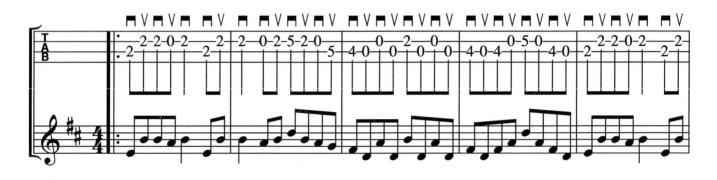

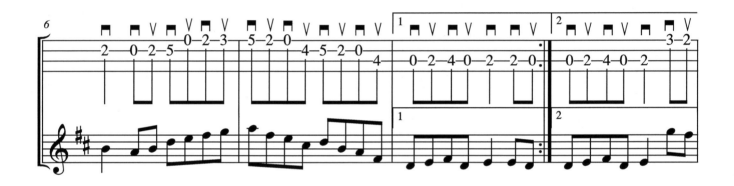

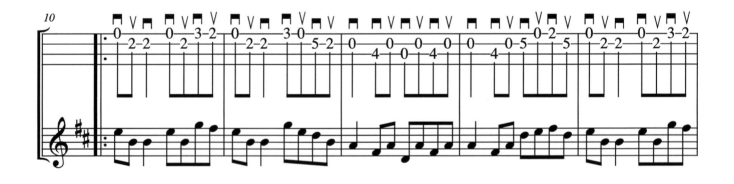

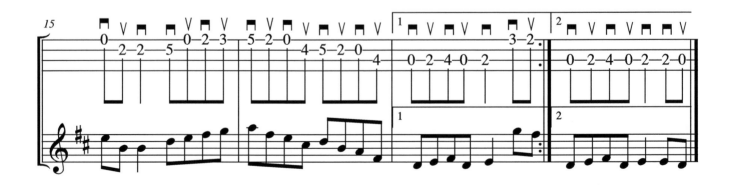

**Reel Set 3 - Tune 2** In measures 3, 7 and 15, the first-finger rolls or barres over the first and second string.

35

# The Maid Behind the Bar
## Judy's Reel - The Barmaid

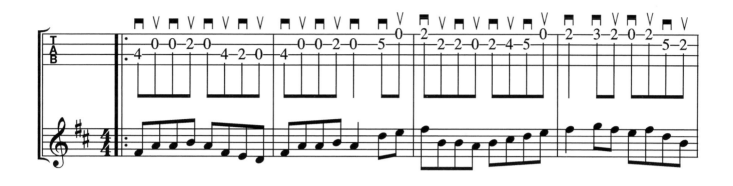

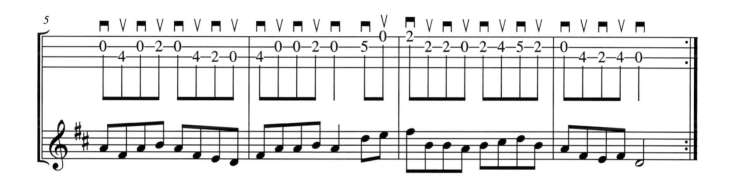

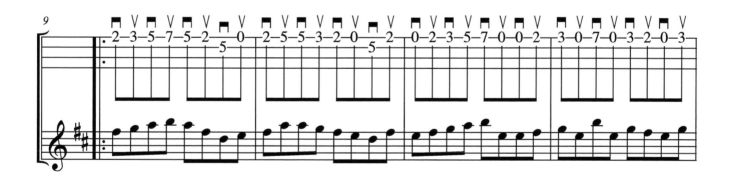

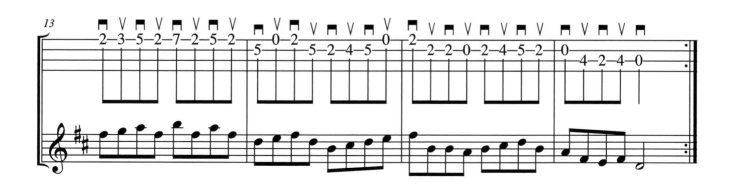

**Reel Set 3 - Tune 3** Measures 4 and 13 include the first-finger barre or roll.

# The Wise Maid

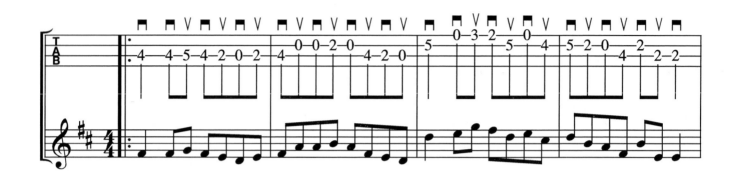

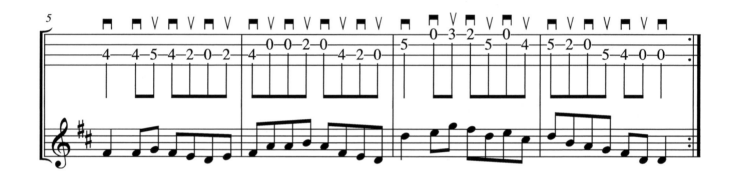

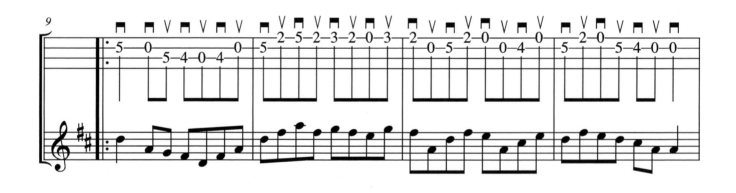

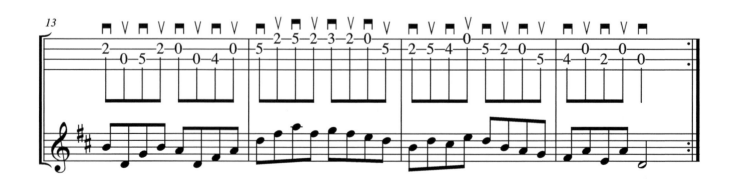

**Reel Set 4 - Tune 1** Notice the quarter notes in measures 1, 2, 5, 7, 9, 10, 13 and 14. These are notes that can be ornamented. Basic ornamentation will be explained later. Measures 1, 2 and 5 use the first-finger roll from the 2nd to 3rd string.

# The Drunken Landlady

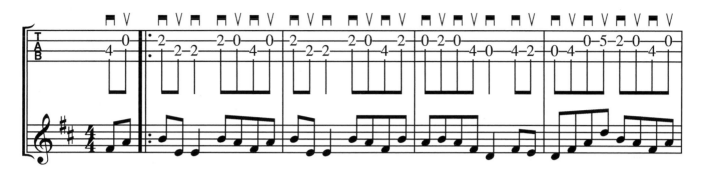

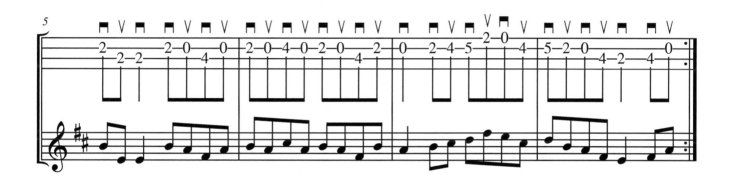

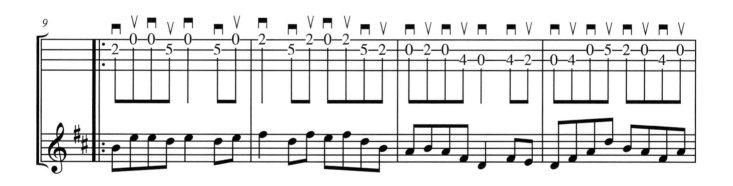

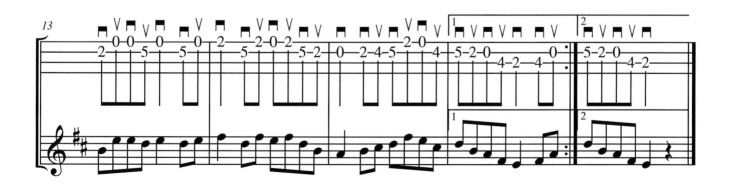

**Reel Set 4 - Tune 2** Note the use of the fourth finger in the turn.

# The Bird in the Bush
## The Bird in the Tree

 38

**Jig Set 3** Here is the first of a two-jig set. In measure 7, we have another basic ornament, as on page 21 in the tune *Boys of the Town*.

 39

# The Geese in the Bog

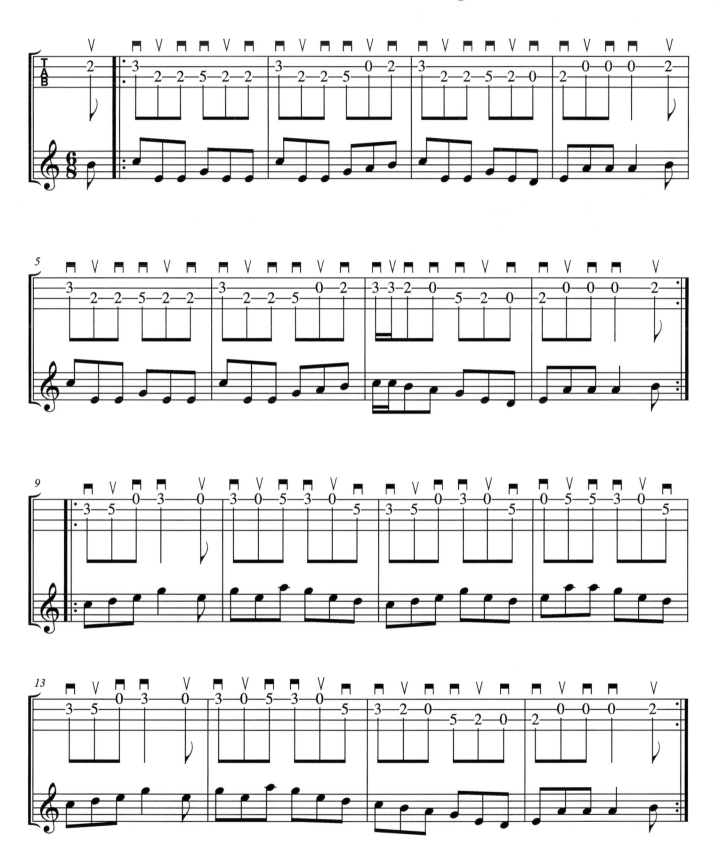

**Jig Set 3 – Tune 2** - When making the transition from *The Geese in the Bog* to *The Pipe on the Hob*, don't play the B note in the last measure of *Bog*. Either replace it with another A note or allow the previous A note to sustain until the first measure of *Hob*. Listen to the CD.

 40

# The Pipe on the Hob

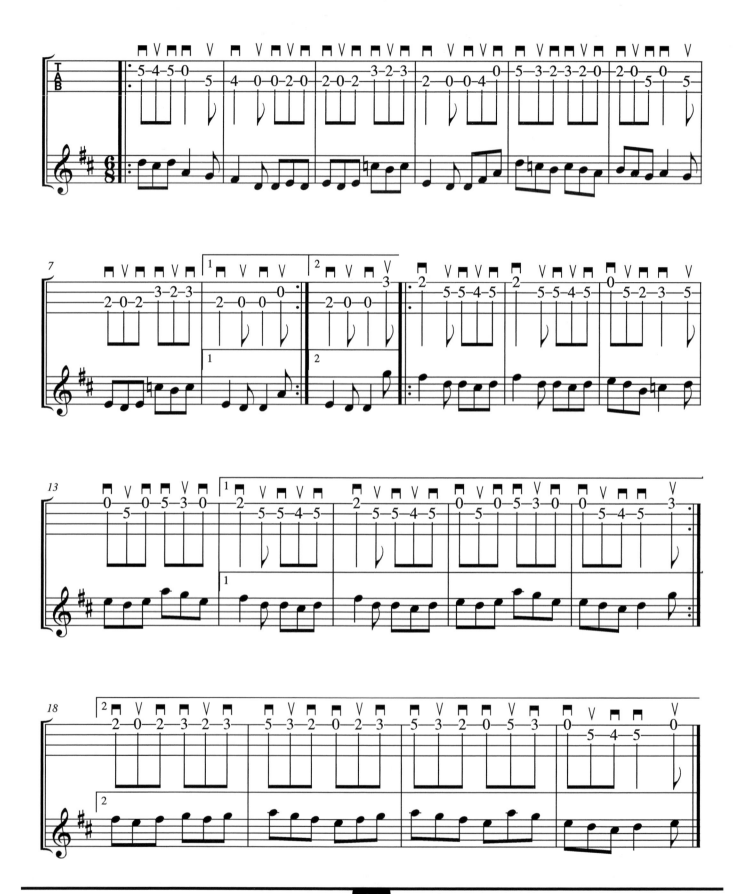

# Ornamentation and Melodic Variation

Ornamentation and melodic variation are important features of Irish music. While some books present these elements from the beginning, the authors feel beginners are better served with a good basic grounding in proper pick direction and a solid understanding of the body of the tunes in this volume rather than learning (at a much slower pace) a few tunes presented with full ornamentation and melodic variation. With a basic repertoire of tunes, the student will be more prepared to make music with others than if he/she only knows a few tunes. These tunes, played as written, will sound appropriate in session settings where ornamentation is not heard well. In small groups or in solo performance, players will want to add ornamentation to produce a more "Irish" sound.

The primary Irish ornamentation of plectral instruments is the picked triplet or "treble." Included are the tenor banjo, guitar, cittern and mandolin family instruments such as the mandola, bouzouki, octave mandolin (called "tenor mandola" in the UK) and of course, the mandolin.

The picked triplet generally lasts the length of a quarter note. The triplet often consists of three notes of the same pitch although the pitches can change. The rhythm of the triplet is best represented by two sixteenth notes followed by an eighth note. While some variation in technique exists, most players perform the triplet with a DUD motion of the pick. Try the four beat exercise below paying careful attention to the pick direction symbols.

 41

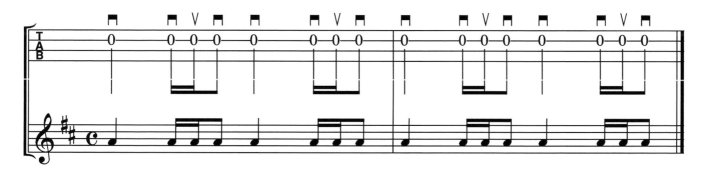

Here are the first two measures of *The Keel Row*. We can see examples of how quarter notes can be replaced by trebles. Review the book looking for quarter notes that can be effectively replaced by trebles. Be aware that Irish players do not play every quarter note as a treble. Variation keeps the music interesting.

 42

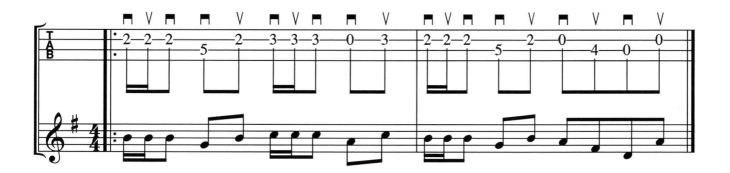

# 43

# The Silver Spear
## Ornamented Version

Here is an ornamented version of an earlier tune. Practice each ornamented measure slowly, paying strict attention to the picking symbols. At faster speeds the triplet will become a quick flick of the pick hand. Memorize this arrangement but realize that an Irish musician varies a tune each time it is played.

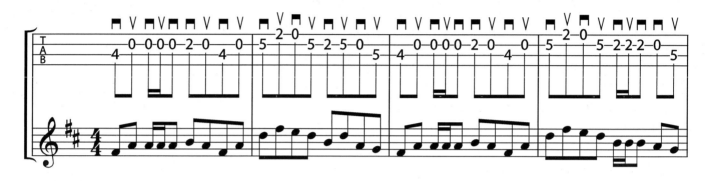

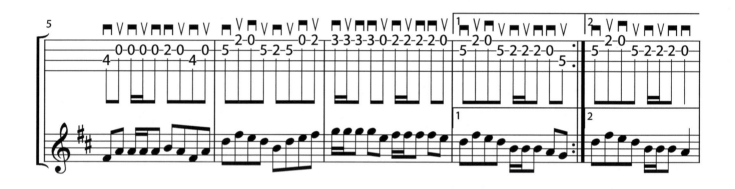

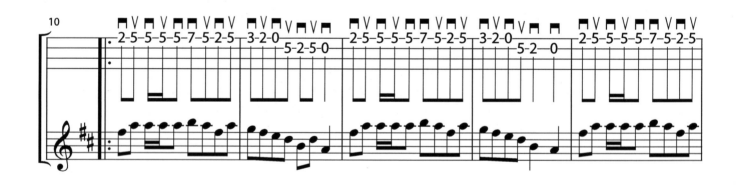

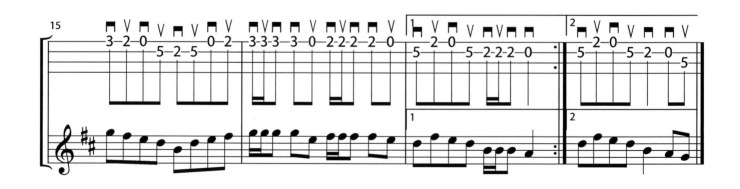

# The Drunken Landlady

## Ornamented Version

 44

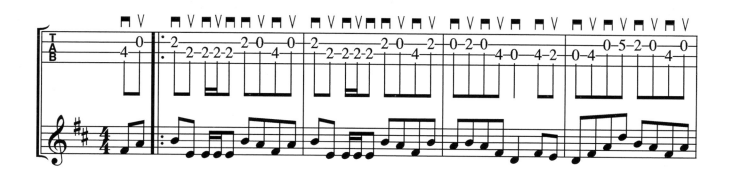

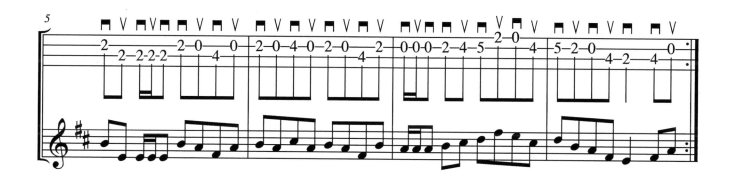

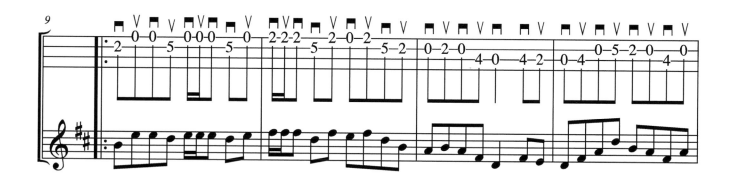

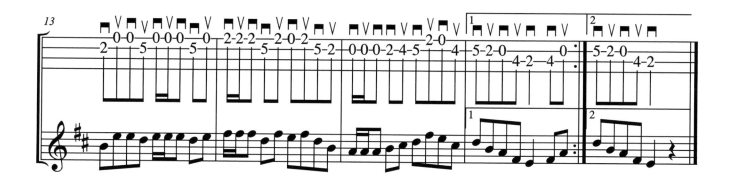

# Conclusion

If you have worked on all the music in this book, you are well on your way to becoming a competent Irish style mandolin player. A serious student of Irish music will commit many years of study to become a good player. A successful session musician's repetroire may include 200 to 500 common tunes. For further study consider the Dave Mallinson books (*100 Enduring Irish Session Tunes, 100 Vital Irish Session Tunes, 100 Essential Irish Session Tunes, 100 Evergreen Irish Session Tunes, 100 Irish Polkas*) available from Mel Bay Publications. Good luck on your fun journey!

**Joe Carr** is a self-taught musician who started guitar at age 13. After six years touring with Alan Munde in the internationally acclaimed bluegrass group *COUNTRY GAZETTE*, Joe left to join the music faculty in the unique commercial music program at South Plains College in Levelland, Texas.

Today, in addition to teaching, Joe continues to produce instructional materials for Mel Bay including *Getting Into Flatpicking Guitar, Getting into Country Guitar, Great Mandolin Picking Tunes* and others. He writes regular columns for *Flatpicking Guitar Magazine* and *Mandolin Magazine*. He is the editor of the webzine *Mandolin Sessions* at http://www.melbay.com/mandolinsessions. Joe's fondness for Irish music extends to mandolin fiddle, tenor banjo and C#/D accordion.

# About the authors

**Michael B. Gregory** is a retired mathematics professor who worked for 35 years at the University of North Dakota. He taught himself to play guitar at the age of 32 and began the mandolin one year later. He has been involved with bluegrass, old-time music and now is dedicated to traditional Irish music on the mandolin.

In 2002, he took up the C#/D Irish button accordion. He spends his time participating in Irish music sessions, learning Irish session tunes, writing mandolin materials for beginners (http://www.melbay.com/mandolinsessions) and in 2006, he took up the art of building mandolins. Michael performs the music on the accompaning CD and plays a mandolin made by Lloyd G. LaPlant of Grand Rapids, Minnesota and various vintage Gibson mandolins.

Michael thanks Jackie Daly for permission to include many tunes taught in his accordion classes at Augusta (2004) and East Durham (2005-6). He also thanks Marla Fibish for teaching him The Drunken Landlady.